Family Walks
in Gower

Amanda Green

Scarthin Books of Cromford
Derbyshire
1993

Family Walks in Gower

Series General Editor: Norman Taylor

The Country Code

Enjoy the countryside and respect its life and work
Guard against all risk of fire
Fasten all gates
Keep your dogs under close control
Keep to public paths across farmland
Use gates and stiles to cross fences, hedges and walls
Leave livestock, crops and machinery alone
Take your litter home
Help to keep all water clean
Protect wildlife, plants and trees
Take special care on country roads
Make no unnecessary noise

Walking the routes in this book

All the routes in this book have been walked, in most cases, several times prior to publication and we have taken great care to ensure that they are on rights of way. However, changes occur all the time in the landscape; should you meet any obstructions, please let us know. Serious obstructions can be brought to the attention of the local branch of the Ramblers Association and the Rights of Way section of the County Council.

Published by Scarthin Books of Cromford, Derbyshire 1993

Printed in Great Britain at The Alden Press, Oxford

ISBN 0907758 630

Cover illustration by Andrew Ravenwood: Three Cliffs Bay (Routes 4 and 8)

Oxwich Wood (Route 11)

Dedication

For Mum, Dad, Tess and Georgie

Acknowledgements

I would like to express my grateful thanks to Kate and John Robson for all their valuable help and advice; to Elizabeth Dyson for her unstinting support and encouragement throughout my time in Gower; to Isobel Thomas for her interest and extensive local knowledge and to Lisa ap Rhydderch for her assistance. My gratitude also goes to John Baldwin for his generous legal advice. Many thanks to Robert Taylor, the County Footpaths' Officer, for his special knowledge of Gower's footpaths, also to Mr Williams, Director of Environment and Highways, and Jonathon Mullard, the Heritage Coast Officer, for their help. I thank Nigel Ajax Lewis of the Glamorgan Wildlife Trust, who gave me much appreciated advice on Gower's wildlife. I would also like to thank the staff of Gower's National Trust and Countryside Council for Wales offices, Pennard Golf Club, and Bryan Pulford of the Forest Enterprise for all their valuable help and co-operation with the many walks over land concerning them. Finally, I thank Pam and Ron for testing the walks, my dog, Tess, for being my companion in Gower, and my dear parents for all their help and for putting up with me while I wrote this guide.

Preface

Gower is a paradise for walkers. Relatively untouched by man, the peninsula retains its natural glory. The scenery is both spectacular and varied, ranging from secluded wooded valleys to open, heather-clad moorland and wild, rugged coastline. The skies are wide and the sea is moody, between them they can change the colour and tone of any scene within minutes.

The climate is mild and sunny, and usually there is an invigorating salt-edged breeze. It is relatively easy walking country with a strong network of footpaths. Much of it is still inaccessible – except by foot. This ensures that even at the height of the tourist season, there are plenty of places – craggy inlets, clear gurgling woodland streams and stretches of golden sand, which are quiet and even deserted.

Gower is superb for the naturalist. Its varied habitats provide for an astonishing array of flora and fauna and many rare species have been preserved.

About the Author

Born in High Wycombe the author spent much time during her early years walking in and enjoying the natural history of the beech woodland by her home. Amanda Green's great affection for the Welsh countryside developed while studying at the University of Wales. She is now living in Hampshire and pursuing her interests in conservation and wildlife photography.

Contents

Map of the area

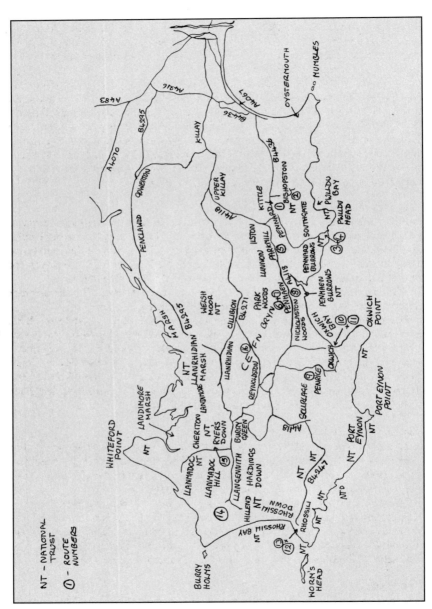

NT – NATIONAL TRUST

① – ROUTE NUMBERS

Introduction

These routes have been selected to cater for families looking for a few hours' quiet walk in glorious countryside, rather than for experienced ramblers hungering for a day-long hike. The routes are all circular and are spread over most of Gower with some in the quieter northern part.

At the back of the book I have made a personal assessment of the difficulty of each route. Walking uneven and slippery country tracks can be quite arduous for little legs, so when selecting a route, do not be over-ambitious with inexperienced youngsters and always be prepared to turn back if necessary. A pace of one mile per hour for younger children is a fair average when estimating how long a route will take, increase it to two miles per hour for experienced 10 and 11-year olds. Allow plenty of time to rest, and for play and exploring. Most of these routes, except the very shortest, are intended to take half a day or longer.

The guide

Directions have been given on how to reach the start of each walk, and where possible I have suggested suitable parking places. Gower does have a bus service and brief details are given where appropriate, but unfortunately it does not touch every route. All details refer to the SWT bus service from Swansea. However, the service is changing and is likely to be reduced by the time of publication.

There is usually a pub or tea room either en route or at the end. Remember that tea rooms vary their opening times according to the time of year.

I am indebted to a number of books concerning Gower. I have listed these, along with a few others which may be of interest to readers, at the end of this guide.

The maps used in conjunction with the directions should be quite adequate. However the 1:25,000 Ordnance Survey Pathfinder maps are always useful. Sheet 1126 covers North Gower and sheet 1145 covers South Gower while a new "Gower" Pathfinder, which combines the two, is currently on trial. Sheet 159 of the 1:50,000 Landranger series covers the whole of Gower.

Clothing and accessories

Walking boots or stout shoes and thick socks are the most sensible footwear for any walker. Many of the routes are damp and muddy even in summer. It is a good idea to take some spare clothes. Light waterproofs are essential: even if it doesn't rain they provide good protection against the cool winds.

If you are taking your own food, please remember to take your litter home – a thoughtlessly dropped can or plastic bag can cause terrible suffering to wildlife and farmstock as well as looking unsightly. Older children may like to use a compass and finally, a pair of binoculars really add to the interest of a walk, especially in an area such as Gower with so much wildlife and superb, far-reaching views.

Out Walking

These walks are largely along rights of way or permissive footpaths. I have usually mentioned the latter in the route concerned and you will often find that it is on land owned by a public body, which maintains a policy of public access. The routes are frequently through National Trust land or a National Nature Reserve. Gower is particularly rich in flora and fauna; please help to keep it that way. It is easy to disturb wildlife without realizing it; try walking quietly, or even sitting still for a while – you stand far more chance of seeing something exciting!

The 'wild' ponies roam freely, although they do have owners. Please don't feed them; if they learn to expect food from people, and don't always get it, they may become frustrated and no longer be gentle, passive animals. There are also a great many sheep in Gower, often roaming freely with the ponies. If you have a dog, please keep him or her under strict control and on a lead at all times. The Gower residents are very friendly towards tourists, but the influx of large numbers of people into such a small area does bring problems. Consideration towards the locals will be much appreciated

I have kept these walks away from traffic whenever possible, but inevitably the odd stretch of road is unavoidable. Traffic can be heavy and fast in Gower, take extreme care when you are on a road, however quiet it seems. The caves are often difficult of access and even dangerous to the inexperienced. In sea caves you can easily be cut off by a rising tide. If you wish to visit the caves, it is worth seeking extra information and essential to always get local advice before you go. Quarries are dangerous, keep well away from them. The route may take you along the top of cliffs, on loose, uneven or steep ground, by the sea or by a stream: at all times walk with common sense, take great care and enjoy your walk!

Natural history

The immense variety of plant and animal life present in Gower is derived from the amazing range of habitats contained within the area. These include sandy and rocky shorelines, clifflands, sand dunes, salt and freshwater marshes, scrub, woodland, streams and ponds, farmland and moorland. It is a naturalist's paradise!

In 1956, Gower was designated Britain's first Area of Outstanding Natural Beauty, and in 1973, 34 miles of coastline were classified as Heritage Coast. The aim of both the AONB and Heritage Coast is to conserve the landscape and its wildlife, while ensuring that people enjoy the area without damaging it.

Virtually all of the coastline is now a nature reserve, but much of it, especially in the south, is still grazed by sheep. Strong winds and salt-laden air generally inhibit plant growth, but many species adapt. The clifflands provide both acidic soils and limestone rock, enabling a tremendous mixture of plants to grow; while the warm and dry nature of the soil, together with the mild climate allows a variety of species from sunnier climes to establish themselves. Trees do not survive well in exposed areas, but gorse, juniper and bracken form scrub, along with hawthorn and blackthorn which are just able to withstand the strong winds.

During the spring and summer, the fine turf is sprinkled with colour from plants such as the delicate, mat-forming spring cinquefoil, horseshoe and kidney vetch, bloody cranesbill, common and hoary rock rose, heather, rock and golden samphire and the brilliant blue flowers of the spiked speedwell. Herb varieties include the scented marjoram and basil thyme. Several spurges, including the Portland variety, inhabit Gower. Stonecrops spread over the rocky ledges, while scurvy grass, bird's foot trefoil and shining cranesbill are often found in the crevices. The orange litchen, Xanthoria, grows on the sun-baked rock itself. Many of these plants common in Gower are much rarer in the rest of Britain, while yellow whitlow grass, found on rocks and walls, occurs only in Gower.

Noisy stonechats frequent the gorse, along with yellowhammers and linnets. Rock and meadow pipits may well be seen, and possibly, near seeding thistles, the colourful goldfinch. Green woodpeckers consider ants a delicacy and venture into the open to investigate their hills. Kestrels commonly hover overhead, and just occasionally that magnificent hunter, a peregrine falcon, may sweep along the cliffs.

Along the shorelines lesser black-backed, great black-backed and herring gulls predominate. Cormorant and fulmar nest in the cliffs, while razorbill, kittiwake, shag and guillemot are most likely to be seen around Worm's Head. The rare chough which hasn't nested in Gower for many years, appeared in 1990, and it is hoped that it will stay to breed. Waders include oystercatchers along with the winter visitors, turnstone, dunlin, knot, sanderling and purple sandpiper. These are often seen around the Burry Estuary and Whiteford Sands where lapwing, curlew and common redshank may be found.

The saltmarshes in the north and south give between them a winter home to a variety of duck, as well as to brent geese, Bewick's, mute and whooper swans. Vegetation in these areas includes glasswort, sea-poa, sea pink, sea lavender and the attractive marsh mallow.

Sand dunes are a haven for botanists. Marram and sea-couch grass help to stabilize the shifting sands. Dewberry is common, as is sea spurge, sea rocket and hairy hawkbit. The large yellow flowers of the tall evening primrose stand out with the brilliant blue of the viper's bugloss and the striking sea holly. In the moist dune slacks, creeping willow often grows with water mint, marsh pennywort and perhaps, fen orchid.

Ash and sycamore dominate the Gower limestone woodlands, but poplar, beech, field maple, hornbeam, hazel, elder and holly also thrive, while willow and alder colonise damp areas. In May and June bluebell-drenched woodlands may also have carpets of the white flowered wild garlic. Primroses, lesser celandines, dog and sweet violets, golden saxifrage, anenomes and wood sorrel flower earlier, while red campion flowers throughout the summer. The delicate enchanter's nightshade flourishes in shady spots. The damp nature of the Gower woodland encourages the growth of ferns, and in rock-strewn areas varieties include soft shield, broad buckler and hart's-tongue fern, while on tree trunks grow the common polypody fern.

Most British mammals except deer, inhabit the woodlands, including possibly the rarer species: red squirrel, polecat and otter. At dawn and dusk greater horseshoe, pipistrelle and long-eared bats emerge from or re-enter their roosts. In sunny glades butterflies taste the sweet nectar of the flowers. Varieties include red admiral, peacock, speckled wood, orange tip and hairstreak.

Map symbols

‒‒‒‒‒	Road
= = = = = =	Track
→ ‒ →	The Route
· · · · · · · · ·	Other Paths
‒+‒+‒	Hedge/Fence/Wall
～～～→	Stream/River With Direction of Flow
/ / / /	Cliff or Other Steep Slope
▬	Building
🌳	Trees
+	Church or Chapel
B	Bridge
G	Gate
S	Stile
P	Car-Park or Other Parking Area
②	Number Corresponding With Walk Directions

Bishopston Valley

Outline

Kittle Green – Bishopston Valley – Backingstone Chapel Ruin – St Teilo's
Church – Kittle Green

Summary

A quiet walk through a secluded wooded valley, part of which is along a dried-up
river bed. From a dark underground cavern beside the path can be heard the
growling of subterranean Bishopston Stream, which then surfaces and flows
alongside the path. A shorter variation may be taken if needed.

The section along the river bed is extremely rocky and has no clear path; you
step/scramble from one rock to another. It is only for the sure-footed and may not
be suitable for very young children. Walking boots are essential.

In winter and after prolonged wet weather floodwater in the upper part of the
valley can render the route impassable. Check the ford by Bishopston Church – if
there is water in it the valley is probably flooded. In this case take the winter
variation above the valley floor.

Attractions

As you cross the stream bed and take the path along the valley floor, you soon pass a
disused quarry up to your left. A rocky gorge emerges down the right and you pass
the waterfall at Daw Pit, with its deep basin below. Sometimes dry in summer, the
water can rise dramatically in winter. Take great care as the path becomes extremely
rocky travelling along the stream bed. Silent and enclosed, with deep green mosses
and ferns, this for me is the most beautiful and secretive part of the walk.

Shortly after the path leaves the rocky bed, you hear the unmistakeable thunder
of subterranean water coming from 'Guthole' or 'Guzzlehole'. Past this, look up to
your left to see the Long Ash silver-lead mine, active in the late eighteenth century.
Where the stream surfaces, look for grey wagtails on exposed rocks in summer. The
stepping stones and bridge provide a short-cut. As you continue, the stream
meanders away from the path which becomes a wide grassy walk along the valley
floor. In summer it comes alive with buzzing insects and feckless butterflies – an
ideal picnic spot.

A steady but clear climb out of the valley brings you to a path with high steps in
places, passing Backingstone Chapel, a small thirteenth century ruin of a monk's
cell, and also on your right, the ruin of Chantry Acre, a large house destroyed by
fire. At a seat and railings, views extend for nearly the whole of the valley from
Kittle to the coast. To the south west, where it twists sharply, sited on a spur
overlooking the valley, is an Iron Age promontory fort. Look out for buzzards
circling above the trees.

Route 1

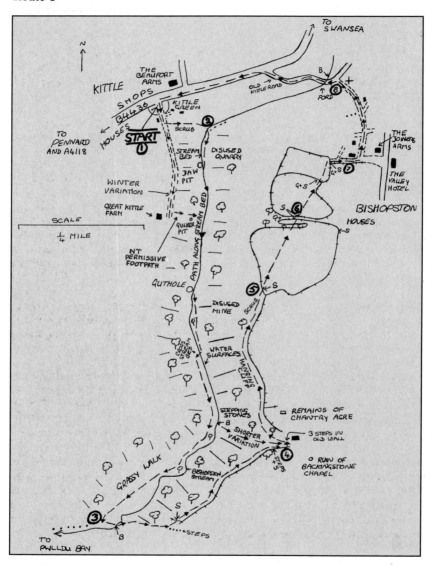

Route 1
Bishopston Valley

$2\frac{1}{2}$ miles)
(shorter variation $1\frac{3}{4}$ miles)

Start

Kittle is situated along the B4436. From the A4118, take the turning south signposted for Bishopston, one mile east of Parkmill. Park with care in Kittle. The route begins at the small Kittle green opposite the bakery and Post Office (GR 574893).

1. Walk across the green towards the valley and continue past the National Trust sign at the far end. Just past a white house on the right is a narrow path to the left; take it, and wind steeply down through scrub to the valley floor.

2. Cross the stream bed (if it is not dry take the winter variation) and turn right along the adjacent footpath. A gorge emerges down to your right. Pass Daw Pit on your right and walk carefully as the path becomes the rocky stream bed. Pass Guthole on your right and continue with the stream bed now on your right and yourself on a much easier, wider path through trees. After a while the path suddenly and clearly drops down and crosses the stream bed so it is now on your left. Soon the water surfaces and the stream bed is filled. Pass stepping stones and a bridge, continue through trees as the path leaves the stream to become wide and grassy.

3. Rejoining the trees, you find the stream. Turn left crossing the bridge and bear left up this short stretch of bridleway as it climbs steadily. Where it forks, take the left-hand path and cross the stile; from here, follow the path as it undulates along the top of the valley, with steps in places.

4. When you are joined by a path ascending from the valley floor on your left, you can make a detour up steps on the right, to a stile and field in which lie the overgrown remains of Backingstone Chapel. Return down the steps. Cross the track from the valley floor and climb 3 steps in an old wall to take the continuation of your original path. After some way, a seat and railings indicate a hanging cliff; take care here!

5. Continue until having passed through scrub, you reach a stile leading into a field. Cross the stile and make towards the middle of what appears to be a hedge lying ahead to your left (do not go towards the houses visible beyond the end of it). The 'hedge' reveals itself to be a belt of trees; take the path which enters it. Descend to a grassy area and at the bottom end of it cross the bar stile in the wall opposite; then turn right along the path, bearing left through trees to another stile.

6. Cross this stile and walk towards the middle of the hedges opposite, reaching the hedge where it bends. Now walk with the hedge on your right. Cross the stile beside a gate into the next field, keep the hedge on your right and exit over another stile.

Continued on page 14

13

7. *Walk up the grassy lane, then continue ahead on a gravel track between two walls. The Joiners Arms lies ahead if you require refreshments! Turn left where the wall and buildings on your left stop, and follow the track which descends, passing a house on your left. Go straight over a cross track and continue descending along a track which has two parallel strips of concrete for vehicles. Go straight over at a second cross track and, still descending, reach St. Teilo's Church.*

8. *Turn left out of the churchyard into Old Kittle Road and cross the ford or footbridge. After a steep climb you reach the main road; turn left and, passing the Beaufort Arms, you reach Kittle green.*

Shorter variation

As for 1 to the stepping stones and bridge in 2, then: cross the bridge over the stream and take the path ahead up the side of the valley to rejoin the route at point 4, where you will be on the path described as ascending from the valley floor.

Winter variation

Cross Kittle green to pass the National Trust sign at the far end, and pass also on your left a path leading down to the valley floor. Continue along the track to Great Kittle Farm. Just before the farm buildings turn left on to a little path which runs down through the woodland to the valley floor. This path is not a right of way but is a National Trust permissive footpath. About three-quarters of the way down you pass on the right Gulver Pit, which has a chestnut paling fence around it. The path reaches the valley floor. Turn right along the stream bed and re-join the route part of the way along point 2.

Public Transport

SWT operates a regular service to the Beaufort Arms.

Refreshments

The Joiners Arms is en route towards the end of the walk. The Beaufort Arms near Kittle green has a garden. Both admit children.

Brandy Cove and Lower Bishopston Valley

Outline
Pyle Corner – Brandy Cove – Pwlldu Bay – Lower Bishopston Valley –
Pyle Corner.

Summary
A quiet lane leads to the coastal path with magnificent views on a clear day across
the Bristol Channel to the North Devon and Somerset coast, and to Lundy Island.
The route runs westward encountering two picturesque bays before returning via
the woodland paths of the lower Bishopston Valley, with its meandering stream.

Pwlldu Bay is pebbly but sandy when the tide is out, making it an ideal spot for
games and a picnic.

The woodland path is particularly uneven, steep and slippery in places. The cliff
path can also be rocky. Children need to be sure-footed and walking boots are
strongly advised. An escape route is available or someone can fetch the car.

Attractions
The name Brandy Cove suggests, and probably originated in, the eighteenth
century smuggling history of this pretty inlet. The raised beach is of the Pleistocene
epoch when the sea was much higher than it is today. From the cliffs above, if it is
clear, look across the Bristol Channel to the coastline of North Devon and Somerset
and to Lundy Island.

The narrow lane from the cliff car-park provides an escape route back to Pyle
Corner.

Pwlldu (pronounced 'Pullth Dee') means dark/black pool. Without road access,
this is another quiet bay. It, too, has a smuggling history, reputed to have been
active at the eighteenth century Beaufort Arms, which was one of the buildings
beside the bay. The (quarried) limestone pebble storm beach dams the Bishopston
stream, forming a pool. Scars of extensive nineteenth century limestone quarrying
are still visible along the side of Pwlldu Head.

In Bishopston Valley notice the mossy green tree trunks, ferns and fungi, which
enhance the impression of damp, rich woodland. Hazel, ash, beech, holly,
hawthorn and small-leaved lime, which is rare in Gower, line the path while the
stream meanders over to your right. Listen out for the cries of buzzard, as well as the
laughing call of the green woodpecker. Near the stream look out for kingfishers.
You ascend a bridleway leaving the valley; the final section follows quiet lanes.

Refreshments
Ideally take a picnic. There is a shop at Pyle Corner, and The Joiners Arms is about
half a mile along the Bishopston Road with The Beaufort Arms in Kittle. Both
admit children.

15

Route 2

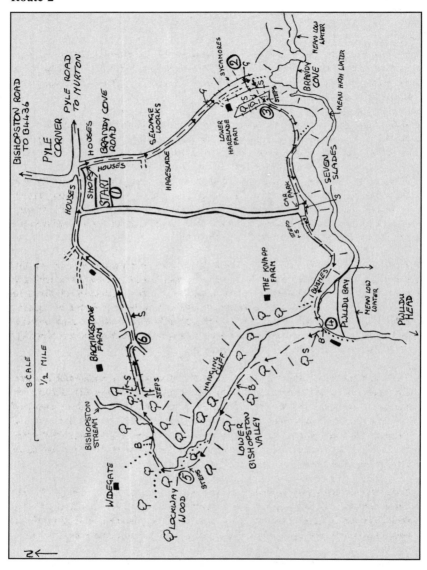

Route 2
Brandy Cove and Lower Bishopston Valley   3 miles

Start

Pyle Corner is situated just south of Bishopston village. From the B4436 take the turning south signposted for Bishopston, just east of Kittle. Pyle Corner is the sharp left-hand bend after three-quarters of a mile. Turn off at this bend and park with care (GR 581883).

1. *Walk down Brandy Cove Road passing the sewage works; here tarmac gives way to gravel. Go through a kissing-gate beside a metal gate, into a track with sycamores up to the left. Pass Lower Hareslade Farm on the right.*

2. *Go through another kissing-gate and walk straight ahead if you wish to visit Brandy Cove. To continue the route, take the path to the right (just after the kissing-gate), down the bank and over a stile into a field. Cross straight to a second stile leading into a wooded area. Where the path forks, go right, up a steep flight of steps to the top of the cliff. Brandy Cove is down to your left.*

3. *Turn right along the path beside the hedge, with a rough area to your left. On meeting the path from around the cliff edge, turn right along it. After a while the path becomes rocky – take care, and it descends to a small car-park on the right with a stile into it. The lane from here forms a short cut back to Pyle Corner, turn right at the end. The path descends to a stile at the far end of this car-park, cross it and go down the steps, turning left into a bridleway which leads to Pwlldu. Turn left at the bottom if you wish to visit Pwlldu Bay.*

4. *The route itself continues straight on. Cross the bridge over the Bishopston Stream, turn right, and shortly cross the stile by the National Trust sign, into Bishopston Valley. The path is stony and often slippery in places, so take particular care in bad weather. You cross a wooden bridge which runs parallel with, but not over, the stream. Where the path forks, go left up through the trees away from the flat, often wet, valley floor. Here the path is steep, uneven and slippery and with the aid of steps rejoins the stream.*

5. *Turn left and follow the track as it bears right; pass several paths leading off to the left, and then cross the bridge over the stream. You are now on a bridleway for the rest of the route. Bear left as the track climbs steadily; when it forks, go right up steps, straight to the top of the valley and into a hedge-bordered lane.*

6. *The lane emerges into a narrow road, turn left along it and follow it, with care, back to Pyle Corner.*

Public Transport

SWT service regularly stops at the Valley Hotel. From here you would have to walk about half a mile along the road to Pyle Corner.

Foxhole Bay (Route 3)

4 miles
(easier variation $3\frac{1}{2}$ miles)

Pwlldu Head and Lower Bishopston Valley

Outline
Southgate – Pwlldu Head – Lower Bishopston Valley – Hael – Southgate

Summary
A particular favourite of mine, this walk encompasses a long, refreshing ramble along a spectacular and blowy stretch of coastline, passing two important bone caves. This is followed by the peace of the woodland and stream in the beautiful Bishopston Valley. A quiet lane returns to the start.

The blustery, exposed Pwlldu Head is wonderfully exhilarating, but having descended from the Head you then have a long steep climb up steps back to the top of the cliff. A short cut through a lane avoids this part. Some sections are uneven, steep and slippery in places. There is also an extremely muddy lane to cross. Walking boots are advised and children need to be sure-footed.

Attractions
Minchin Hole, reached from Foxhole Bay, is Gower's largest bone cave. Remains found include those of elephant, soft-nosed rhinoceros, bear, hyena, and unusually, lion. There is evidence of occupation in Roman times and during the Dark Ages.

East of Foxhole Bay is Hunts Bay and Bacon Hole. Hunts Bay, otherwise known as Deepslade, gets its name from the nearby farm which was given by William le Breos, the Norman Lord of Gower, to his huntsman, William de Hunde. Bacon Hole is situated in the cliffs just west of Hunts Bay and is named from horizontal bands of dark red just inside it. These are most likely due to mineral seepage (probably red oxide), but were originally thought to have been painted by early inhabitants. Remains of soft-nosed rhinoceros, elephant, giant ox, wolf and reindeer have been found there. Human occupation existed in the Iron Age, Roman times and later.

Beware of strong winds on Pwlldu Head which rises to 300 feet (91 m). As you walk out on to the headland you pass the remains of an Iron Age fort and pottery. During the nineteenth century limestone was quarried extensively on the east side and exported to the North Devon coast. In 1760 the *Caesar* was wrecked here drowning about 70 press-ganged men who were buried at Gravesend.

After descending Pwlldu Head you have a steep climb up steps to the top of the cliff again. If you wish to visit Pwlldu Bay before entering Bishopston Valley, it is a good place to rest or picnic and at low tide children can play on the sand. For details of Pwlldu Bay and Bishopston Valley, see Route 2.

You turn out of Bishopston Valley and continue through Lockway Wood. The lane you have to cross can be very muddy and difficult, even with boots – good luck! The lane returning to the start via Hael is quiet, but as always, beware of any traffic.

Route 3

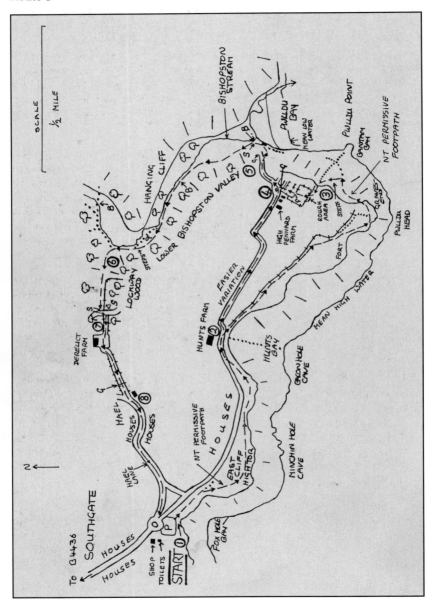

Route 3
Pwlldu Head and Lower Bishopston Valley

(4 miles)
(shorter variation 3½ miles)

Start

The only approach to Southgate is via the B4436. From the A4118 take the turning south signposted for Bishopston, one mile east of Parkmill, then turn right at the junction for Southgate. The road ends at Pennard Cliffs; park in the National Trust car-park there (GR 554874). An attendant is not always present, but contributions towards the excellent work done by the National Trust are always welcome and a box is provided.

1. *Facing the sea, leave the car-park in the far left-hand corner along the wide, grassy track leading on to National Trust property at East Cliff. After a little way turn right towards the cliff edge. This part of the walk from point 1 to point 2 is not along a right of way, but is a National Trust permissive route. Walk east along the cliffs towards Hunts Bay and Bacon Hole. The track bears left around the bay and joins a tarmac road in front of the houses. Turn right at the road and pass Hunts Farm on your left. A path leads down to the bay, if you wish to visit it.*

2. *From Hunts Farm take the track ahead beside an overgrown wall and fence on the left. When the wall bends sharply left and the path forks, go right, out on to Pwlldu Head. On the far side of the headland, the path turns in towards the wall and forks. Take the right-hand fork, a wide grassy track off the headland through gorse and bracken. Descend and then take the steps up to the left which lead to the top of the cliff. This part of the route, from the track over Pwlldu Head to the top of the steps, does not follow a right of way, but again is on a National Trust permissive footpath.*

3. *Enter the field at the top and walk straight ahead beside a rough area. After a short distance take the path leading to the right through the rough area, until, bending right through bushes, it reaches two fence posts positioned to allow people, but not stock, through. Cross the field to the gateway and waymark sign opposite. Go through, and across a field with a hedge on your left, through a second pair of posts and cross another field with a variety of young trees planted on the right. A third set of posts leads on to a gravelled drive at a bend. Go straight ahead and through the gate.*

4. *Walk down the lane towards Pwlldu Bay. Before reaching a gate ahead of you, turn right on to the bridleway, and ignore the path off to the left after a few yards. Take care as it winds down; steep, uneven and muddy, it is very slippery in wet weather. With Pwlldu Bay out to the right, turn left on to the track at the bottom leading to Bishopston Valley.*

Continued on page 22

21

5. *Pass a bridge on your right and, after a few yards, cross the stile beside the National Trust sign. Continue, with care, along the stony (and sometimes slippery) path with steep woodland on your left and the winding Bishopston Stream over to your right. You cross a wooden bridge which runs parallel to, but not over, the stream. Where the path forks, go left up through the trees away from the damp valley floor. It is steep, uneven and slippery, and then with the aid of steps this path shortly rejoins the stream; turn left and continue beside it.*

6. *Soon, another valley leads off to the left; turn left on to the bridleway running through it. Having been joined by a fence on the left, you soon reach a lane. Cross the stiles into and out of the lane to reach the bridleway on the other side.*

7. *The bridleway leads up a sunken lane through trees, before widening out with banked hedges and fields on either side. Continue through a derelict farm and leave via the gravel lane to the left (which immediately bends to the right).*

8. *Go through a gate and pass a bungalow on the left before reaching a tarmac road; turn left and walk with care along the road. Continue, and shortly you arrive back at the start.*

Shorter variation
As for 1 to 2 then; follow the lane to Pwlldu to rejoin the route at point 4.

Public Transport
SWT operates a regular service to Pennard Cliffs.

Refreshments
Ideally take a picnic. The Pennard Stores is near the car-park. The Southgate County Club, a short walk back up the road in Southgate, is a members' club, but you can enter if you sign the book. Children are admitted under supervision during the day. Snacks are available but no tea or coffee.

West Cliff and Pennard Castle

Outline
Southgate – West Cliff – Pennard Burrows – Pennard Castle – Golf Links – Southgate

Summary
This easy route starts with a breezy walk along the dramatic coastline of West Cliff towards Pobbles Beach. The route continues above Three Cliffs Bay and the meandering Pennard Pill. Herons are frequently seen here. The highlight of the walk is the splendid ruin of Pennard Castle. The return crosses the sandy golf links and continues along the road through Southgate to the start.

Attractions
As you walk along the cliff top behind you is East Cliff and views ahead encompass Pobbles Beach, Three Cliffs Bay, Great Tor and beyond to Oxwich Bay and Point. To the north west is the village of Penmaen, and behind it is the rise of Cefn Bryn. Notice in spring and summer the wide variety of butterflies and other insects visiting the clifftop flowers.

From the depression at the start of the boardwalk you can visit Pobbles Beach if the tide is out.

Three Cliffs Bay is named from the three limestone points on the east side. The Pennard Pill winds into the sea here, with an area of saltmarsh at the head of the sandy bay. On the west side is an area of highly unstable dunes. Also on the same side rise Penmaen Burrows, on the edge of which once stood the 12th century Penmaen Castle, overlooking the bay.

As the boardwalk turns inland views emerge of the silvery Pennard Pill, the saltmarsh and dunes at the head of the bay, and of the wooded slope across the valley. Remember to look out for herons here.

The Church ruin is a victim of besanding. A thirteenth century church, dedicated to St Mary, it was deserted in the sixteenth century for the present Pennard Church, on a less sandy site. No footpath leads up to this ruin.

Pennard Castle is a late thirteenth century stone castle which has largely collapsed, but its ruin is still formidable standing above a steep-sided valley. The curtain wall on the north side is virtually intact and the twin D-shaped gate towers are striking. The 'keep' which is the square room overlooking the valley, was a later addition to the curtain wall. However, inside, the courtyard is besanded and the hall, a typical example of the period, contained a communal room, a private room and twin service rooms. Its rounded corners may sometimes be seen since it was reburied following excavation in 1961. Pennard Castle was just one of the victims along the South Gower coast of drifting sands, aggravated by storms in the fourteenth century; by 1650 it was abandoned.

23

Route 4

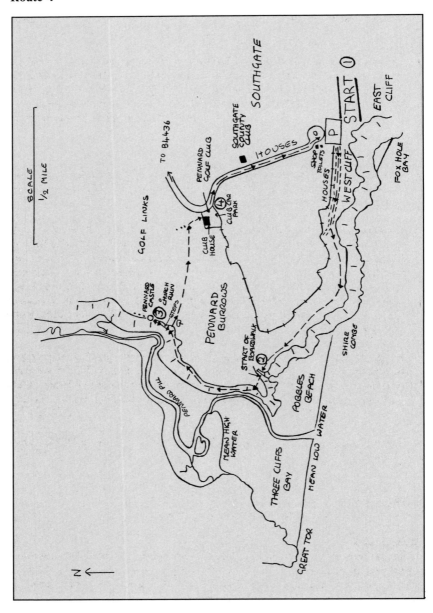

Route 4

West Cliff and Pennard Castle $2\frac{3}{4}$ miles

Start

> *The only approach to Southgate is via the B4436. From the A4118 take the turning south signposted for Bishopston, one mile east of Parkmill, then turn right at the junction for Southgate. The road ends at Pennard Cliffs; park in the National Trust car-park there (GR 554874). An attendant is not always present, but contributions towards the excellent work done by the National Trust are always welcome and a box is provided.*

1. *Turn right out of the car-park along the tarmac road with the sea to your left. When the road comes close to the cliff edge, leave the road and strike out on a fairly central route along the cliff top.*

2. *Go down the track into the depression which leads to Pobbles Beach and up the other side to a sign which asks you to keep to the path beside the golf links. Take the boardwalk which begins here and continues through Pennard Burrows. This boardwalk is not a right of way but the Golf Club has erected it for use by the public. Follow the boardwalk as it turns inland and overlooks the Pennard Pill, and then as it descends into a gully and up steps on the other side. As you continue, the church remains lie just over the burrows on your right, and shortly after, you reach the ruin of Pennard Castle.*

3. *From here, retrace your steps to the gully, turn left along it and follow white stones, passing hawthorn and a ditch on your right. This is part of the golf links so beware of flying golf balls! Near the clubhouse you meet another well used north–south path; turn right on to this to reach the Golf Professional's Shop and the club car-park.*

4. *Turn right and walk with care along the road to the start, passing the Southgate County Club on the left.*

Public Transport
SWT provides a regular service to Pennard Cliffs.

Refreshments
Ideally take a picnic. Near the car-park is the Pennard Stores. The Southgate County Club, which you pass as you return along the road, is a Members' Club but you can enter if you sign the book. Children admitted under supervision during the day. Snacks are available but no tea or coffee.

25

Pobbles Beach and Three Cliffs Bay

Pennard Castle

26

Ilston Cwm

Outline

Parkmill – Ilston Cwm – Ilston – Lunnon – Parkmill

Summary

Perhaps my favourite woodland walk, this little valley with its fast-flowing stream (the Killy-Willy) is totally enchanting. The route runs along the cool, shady valley floor passing the remains of the first Baptist Chapel in Wales. It reaches the delightful village of Ilston, via the churchyard. A quiet, sunny lane and fields provide the setting for a gentle stroll back to the start. If necessary, when you reach the village of Ilston someone can return to fetch the car.

This is an easy route, but right at the end there is a short walk back along the busy A4118 to the start, and there is not pavement all of the way. You can assess this stretch before you begin the walk, you may prefer to send someone to fetch the car while the rest of the party waits closer to the end of section 6.

Attractions

For children who like water, bridges and the game of 'pooh sticks' this walk, with 8 bridges, is paradise. In the secluded, wooded valley you follow pretty Ilston Stream through ash, sycamore and hazel, until you reach the Baptist Chapel ruin.

Built by John Myles, on the site of the medieval Trinity Well Chapel, this was the first Baptist Chapel in Wales, 1649–60. When gatherings of dissenters became illegal in 1663, Myles emigrated to America, where he founded the town of Swansea. A memorial to its founder was erected at the ruin in 1928 and was unveiled by David Lloyd George.

The path crosses another bridge and you stroll on through tall larches, their soft needles scenting the valley floor. Over a bridge and you are now deep in Ilston Cwm, where only the sound of rippling water and birdsong break the intense silence. Notice the variety of mosses and ferns. Another bridge, and you continue through poplars, their paper-thin leaves fluttering in the softest breeze.

Thirteenth-century Ilston Church is built on the site of a monk's cell and is dedicated to St Illtyd – the figure in the stained glass lancet in the north side of the nave. The church was presented to the Knights Hospitallers of St John, in 1221 by John le Breos. One of its rectors was John Myles, founder of the nearby Baptist Chapel. A yew tree in the churchyard is thought to be 600 years old.

A quiet lane leads to Lunnon. Cefn Bryn can be viewed through the gate opposite the T-junction. A track and field complete the circuit to Parkmill.

Refreshments

The Gower Inn at Parkmill admits children, has high chairs and frequently offers a childrens' menu. There is a beer garden.

Route 5

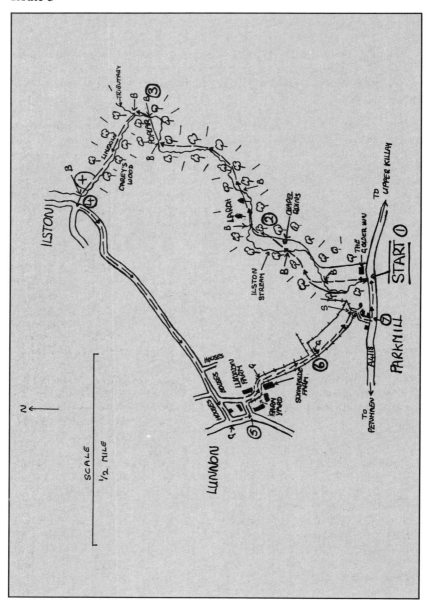

Route 5
Ilston Cwm

2¾ miles

Start

Parkmill is situated on the A4118. The start of the walk is next to The Gower Inn (GR 552891). Parking is difficult, but if you stop for refreshments at The Gower Inn, and ask there, you may be able to use their car-park.

1. *Take the track signposted for Ilston Cwm, on the west side of The Gower Inn; the Ilston Stream is on your left. Soon the path diverges from the stream and crosses a field. Rejoining the stream, cross a bridge, and enter the quiet woodland of the valley. The path is clear, but not too wide. Continue, until the path crosses another bridge. On the right are the ruins of the Baptist Chapel.*

2. *With the stream now on your left, follow the path to a third bridge; cross it and continue through larches. The path crosses another bridge and then another so that the stream is now on your right as you walk through poplars.*

3. *Cross yet another bridge so the stream is now on your left. Shortly, you cross a stone bridge over a tributary, walk straight ahead away from the tributary, and soon you find the main stream on your left. The path continues through the churchyard and then crosses a final bridge over the stream.*

4. *Walk up the track out of the churchyard, then turn left up the tarmac lane (stables opposite). Continue, with care, along this lane for ¾ mile, into the quiet hamlet of Lunnon. Walk on through the hamlet; at the T-junction turn left for Parkmill.*

5. *Take the first lane to the left, by a sign for Lunnon Farm. Where the road bends to the left, turn right beside a signpost for Stonemill; on the right are a wall and farm buildings, with houses opposite. The path then bends left into a grass/concrete lane and quickly bends right again, before continuing straight on with hedges on either side.*

6. *Where the track bends sharply left, go through the gate on the bend and walk straight down the long, narrow field. At the bottom is a tall metal gate, and on the left is a bar stile. Cross this and continue down some steps. Just past a house on the right, the path bends sharply down to the left; here, take the path leading off the bend to the right. This path soon bends sharply left; concrete, steep and narrow, it runs straight down to the main road.*

7. *Turn left, and walk with extreme care along the road past the Girl Guides Activity Centre to the start, or arrange for someone to fetch the car.*

Public Transport
No bus service stops at the start of this route.

Ilston Stream

Park Woods and Green Cwm

Outline

Penmaen – Park Woods – Cathole – Parc le Breos Tomb – Parkmill – Penmaen

Summary

One of my favourites, this cool woodland walk follows wide, easy tracks through to the valley of Green Cwm. Here, a variety of magnificent trees line the grassy margins of the track. Cathole cave is visible in a high rock face, and Parc le Breos chambered tomb is of considerable interest. A tarmac road leads to the Crafts and Countryside Centre in Parkmill. From here the route winds up through leafy Northill Wood and along a hedged bridleway to Penmaen, where its church can be visited.

The hard track along Green Cwm, being relatively dry, makes a good winter walk in itself when done from Parkmill. The path through Northill Wood is uphill, uneven and can be slippery – it requires sure-footed youngsters and walking boots are advised. If there are small or tired members in the family they could wait at the Crafts and Countryside Centre where there are tea rooms, while mum or dad fetches the car.

Attractions

Once on the farm road you look back to glorious views of Oxwich Bay and Point, Penmaen Burrows, Three Cliffs Bay, Pennard Burrows and further east along the coastline to Pwlldu Head and beyond. When you start along the permissive footpath it is possible to see ahead through the trees to the ridge in North Gower.

The grassy margins of Green Cwm are bounded by a variety of ancient trees, with many under preservation orders. The path bends slightly right; look out for Cathole high in a rock face on your left. In 1968 excavations at this bone cave yielded flint blades which suggested human occupation around the end of the last Ice Age. There is also evidence, which includes human remains, of use during Mesolithic times and the Bronze Age.

To your right is Church Hill where there is an undated earth-work. Soon, you pass a restored limekiln on the left and the burial chamber opposite.

Parc le Breos chambered tomb, also known as 'Giants Grave', is a Neolithic chambered tomb built between 4000–3000 BC. The cairn is 24 yards long and excavations in 1869 revealed a passageway and four side chambers, which originally would have been roofed with stone slabs. Used over time as a communal burial site, remains suggest at least 25 people were buried there, and probably many more. Some fragments of Neolithic pottery have also been found. It is likely that it was built on the bank of the stream which now flows underground.

Continued on page 34

Route 6

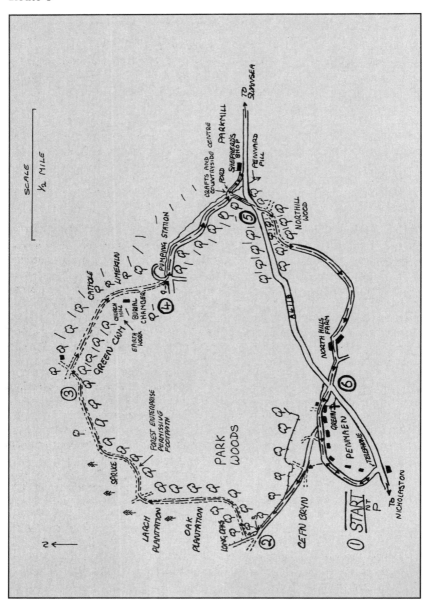

32

Route 6
Park Woods and Green Cwm $3\frac{3}{4}$ **miles**

Start

Penmaen is on the A4118 about one mile west of Parkmill. If travelling westwards, take the road to the right at the western end of Penmaen, just before a small car-park on the left. Leave your car in the National Trust parking area (GR 527885). A contribution towards the important work done by the National Trust is always welcome, and a box is provided.

1. *Turn left up the tarmac road from the National Trust parking area. Where the road bends right, take the track off to the left opposite a house and telegraph pole (the houses on the right reach the road here). This leads up through gorse and heather to a farm road at a point where it bends; turn left along it. Continue along the edge of Cefn Bryn until you reach a stile into the Forest Enterprise Park Woods which you join on your right; 15 yards further on the road forks.*

2. *Cross the stile and follow the narrow path left along the edge of the woodland for a short distance, then bear right with it into a wider track. This part of the route from point 2 to point 3 is not a right of way, but is a permissive footpath, maintained by the Forest Enterprise. Follow the track round to the left. Mature oaks remain on your right, whilst you pass both an oak and a larch plantation on the left. Ignore tracks leading off either side while rounding a wide curve to the right.*

3. *On reaching a cross-track with a seat opposite, turn right on to a broad, hard track through the valley. Pass Cathole, Church Hill, a limekiln and Parc le Breos chambered tomb.*

4. *Go through the gate at the end of the field, near the water pumping station. Turn right out of this, then left down the tarmac road. After half a mile, turn left to the Crafts and Countryside Centre. Shepherd's shop is beyond that.*

5. *Return to the point where you turned left, and turn left; you shortly reach the main road. Take the track opposite, down through a gateway into a grassy area. Follow, with care, the bridleway to the right, which uneven and slippery leads up through Northill Wood. At the top, continue between hedges; after passing North Hills Farm follow the tarmac road through to the main road.*

6. *Cross carefully, it's a difficult spot, and follow the road through the green. You can visit Penmaen Church on the left. Continue with care along the road for half a mile, bearing left until you reach the start.*

Public Transport
SWT provides a fairly regular service to Penmaen.

As you turn on to the tarmac road, the private road to the right leads to Parc le Breos, which was once the hunting estate of the le Breos family, Norman Lords of Gower in the thirteenth and fourteenth centuries. Look out for kingfishers along the stream which has now surfaced on your left.

After the excitement of the tomb, the eyes of young ones will light up still further with the prospect of teas at the Crafts and Countryside Centre! This used to be the mill and is well worth a visit.

As the mature sycamores of Northill Wood give way to fields, look out for buzzards and kestrels circling on either side. This was the original road until early last century.

Refreshments
The Crafts and Countryside Centre at the Old Mill in Parkmill, en route, has tea rooms. Shepherd's shop is also in Parkmill.

Ilston Church (Route 5)

Cefn Bryn

Outline
Penmaen – Cefn Bryn ridge – Nicholaston – Penmaen

Summary
A relatively short, easy walk along Gower's central ridge, returning via the lower slopes. It is a useful route which gives a clear perspective of the peninsula. A clear day is essential for the spectacular views, which stretch from North Devon and Somerset right across the peninsula to the Brecon Beacons, to reach their full potential. Marvellous for a sense of space, it is particularly vivid in August when colourful splashes of gorse and heather adorn the upper slopes.

The hard track along the ridge, though not always dry, still makes a good winter walk. If necessary, tired little ones can wait with an adult at Nicholaston while someone fetches the car.

Attractions
Cefn Bryn ridge, formed of Old Red Sandstone, is centrally positioned, it includes the second highest point in the peninsula 610 ft (186 m), and is a dominant feature justly known as the 'backbone' of Gower. Not surprisingly, it played a major part in the activities of prehistoric man. Archaeological interest includes the famous Arthur's Stone (see route 16) and cairns, built around 3000–2000 BC, are to be found among the bracken. There are also a number of disused quarries on the slopes. The track which this route follows, running the length of Cefn Bryn, is called Talbot's Way; it was used for regular excursions in the last century by the Talbot family of Penrice Castle. Nowadays, 'wild' ponies and sheep graze this area of common land.

A steady incline brings you to a cairn, but you haven't reached the top yet! From here you can look back over the whole of East Gower. To the south lie Penmaen Burrows, Three Cliffs Bay, Pennard Burrows and Castle. The incline lessens and you pass a fenced-off area and the trig point. Views to the south now include Nicholaston Wood, Oxwich Bay and Point. Across the Bristol Channel, the North Devon and Somerset coastline, and Lundy Island are visible on a clear day. Views of North Gower emerge, including Llanrhidian, and on the north ridge, Penclawdd. Llanelli is on the far side of the estuary, with Pembrokeshire's Presceli Hills in the west and the Brecon Beacons to the north east. Westwards lies the shadow of Rhossili Down on the far edge of Gower.

An old cart track leads down to Nicholaston. A grassy bridleway, which can be wet in places, passes through the bracken of the lower slopes, back to Penmaen.

Refreshments
Take a picnic. The nearest tea rooms are at the Crafts and Countryside Centre in Parkmill.

Route 7

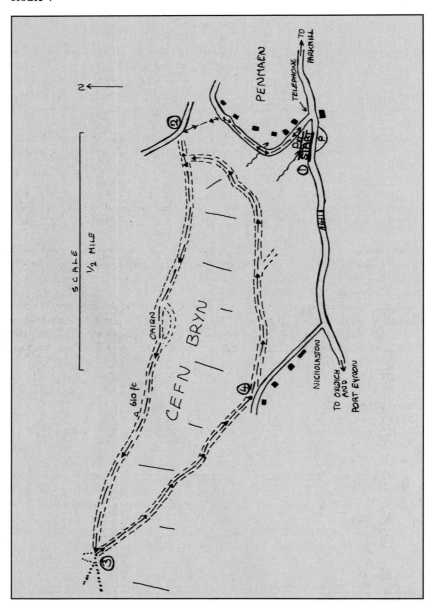

36

Route 7
Cefn Bryn $2\frac{1}{2}$ miles

Start

Penmaen is on the A4118, about one mile west of Parkmill. If travelling westwards, take the road to the right at the western end of Penmaen, just before a small car-park on the left. Leave your car in the National Trust parking area (GR 527885). A contribution towards the important work done by the National Trust is always welcome, and a box is provided.

1. *From the parking area, turn left up the tarmac road which curves gradually to the right. Where the road bends to the right, take the track off to the left opposite a house and telegraph pole (the houses on the right reach the road here).*

2. *Walk up through the gorse and heather to meet a farm road; from here take a wide track, a bridleway, just to the left, which leads up on to Cefn Bryn. After an incline you pass a cairn and a fenced-off area and the trig point. Continue westwards.*

3. *About a third of a mile after the trig point, you reach a meeting point of six tracks. Take the first one to your left, which is an old cart track leading down to Nicholaston.*

4. *At the base of the Bryn, where you meet a tarmac road and houses, take the track to the left indicated by a signpost for Penmaen and follow this grassy bridleway. When it forks clearly, take the left-hand track which carries straight on, and finally bears left up to the original track on to the Bryn; turn right retracing your steps to point 2 and the start.*

Public Transport
SWT operates a fairly regular service to Penmaen.

Gorse in flower

Penmaen Burrows

Outline
Penmaen – Penmaen Burrows – Ringwork – Great Tor – Little Tor –
Nicholaston Burrows – Penmaen

Summary
Walk this short route for its splendid views and archaeological interest, which
includes the site of a Norman castle and an early rabbit farm. A burial chamber and
the besanded ruin of a Norman church are also among the dunes. Much of this walk
does not follow rights of way, but uses permissive paths on the National Trust
property of Penmaen Burrows, please keep to the paths indicated.

This walk is easy for adults and older children, but paths are through scrub,
narrow at times, and have loose sand underfoot for much of the way. Those with
shorter legs should be allowed plenty of time as it can be hard going for them. A
narrow part starts after the short cut option, so can easily be avoided.

Attractions
The very overgrown remains are of an early church, besanded and abandoned in the
fourteenth century. A legend exists of a whole village, 'Stedworlango', being buried
here, but only the church and some gravestones have been excavated.

The burial chamber is a Neolithic tomb which was used for communal burial
and dates from around 3000 BC. It has a central chamber as well as side ones. The
fallen capstone weighs seven tons.

Penmaen Old Castle is a twelfth century ringwork which was abandoned in the
following century. Its defences consisted of an intimidating bank and ditch on the
vulnerable landward side. As you follow the path past the ringwork the wooded
slopes of Oxwich Point and gradually, the sweeping Oxwich Bay itself, come into
view before being eclipsed as you climb towards Great Tor. On a clear day, Lundy
Island and the North Devon and Somerset cliffs are visible.

Pillow Mound, now indistinct, is a man-made rabbit warren. Rabbits were bred
in medieval times for use as winter food.

Leather's Hole is a bone cave penetrating deep into the rock where remains of
mammoth, hyena and wolf have been excavated. Difficult of access, it is sited in the
'camel's hump' adjacent to the dramatic Great Tor. Little Tor can be seen on the far
side of Tor Bay. From the seat at the head of the bay which is below you, the wide
track offers a short cut. Past the disused limekiln you can look back to your left to
see the striking profile of Great Tor and, beyond that, to Three Cliffs and Shire
Combe. Look out for buzzards and kestrels along here. The narrow path undulates
along and when you reach the stone stile you have a full view of Oxwich Bay and
Point, Nicholaston Woods, Crawley Wood is ahead and Nicholaston Burrows are
below.

Route 8

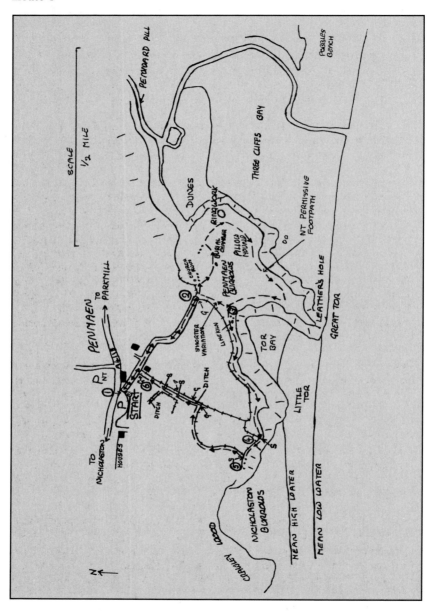

40

Route 8
Penmaen Burrows

2 miles
(shorter variation 1½ miles)

Start

Penmaen is on the A4118 about one mile west of Parkmill. Park in the small car-park at the western end of Penmaen, on your left as you travel westwards. (GR 526884). If this is full, there is a National Trust parking area beside a road virtually opposite; contributions are always welcome, and a box is provided.

1. *From the car-park go through the metal gates into the bridleway signposted for Tor Bay. Continue until finally you reach a gate at the end of the track. Go through this into Penmaen Burrows.*

2. *The route from point 2 to point 3 and part of it to point 4 is along a National Trust permissive footpath. Walk ahead and, after a few yards, where the path forks, there is a small sign on the ground for Tor Bay to the right; go left. After a few more yards you pass a large ash tree on the left. Continue along the main path through the burrows. Soon the path forks clearly, go right. Pass the burial chamber on your right. As you continue, bearing left, Three Cliffs Bay comes into view. When you reach another clear path, turn right along it. You pass the old castle ringwork, a distinctive mound on your left overlooking the bay. Follow the path as it bears right along the cliff tops. Pass Pillow Mound, which is hardly visible, on the right. Continue along the main path, through scrub, well in from, but in line westwards, with the cliff edge. Pass, after a rise, Great Tor. Follow the path around Tor Bay, which is below you, towards the limekiln.*

3. *From the seat at the head of the bay below you, face the limekiln; two narrow paths lead through scrub, the left-hand one descending to Tor Bay. Take the path to the right, which undulates through gorse and bramble, passing the limekiln on the left.*

4. *When you reach a stone stile, cross it. Below to your left are Nicholaston Burrows and ahead is Crawley Wood. Look at the field to your right and ahead you see a hedge in it. The stile over which you enter the field is by that hedge where it meets, at right angles, the hedge with which you are about to walk parallel. Take the narrow, undulating path above the dunes for about 150 yards and look out for a path off to the right and a small bar stile tucked back in the hedge.*

5. *Cross the stile into a field with a wall and fence immediately on your right. Follow this, bearing right, until you meet a hedge and there is a gateway on your right. Turn left and walk with the hedge and ditch on your right. Continue along it in a straight line, encountering two bar stiles, until you reach a gate leading to the lane used on the outward journey, and where a stone building stands on the right.*

6. *Go through the gate and turn left into the lane, retracing your steps to the start.*

Shorter variation
As for 1 to 3 then; from the seat at the head of the bay below you, turn inland along the wide path (a bridleway) which leads to the lane. From there retrace your steps to the start.

Public Transport
SWT provides a fairly regular service to Penmaen.

Refreshments
Take a picnic. The nearest tea rooms are at the Crafts and Countryside Centre in Parkmill.

Penrice Church

Mill Wood and Penrice

Outline
Mill Wood – Mill Ruins – Lake – Penrice – Pennyhitch – Mill Wood

Summary
This short easy walk is through the Forest Enterprise's beautiful Mill Wood with its great variety of trees and plant life. It is particularly glorious in May/June when the rhododendrons are in flower. The ruins of the mill and stew ponds are near the hard track which leads to a lake. This makes an excellent, and dry, winter walk. The still water provides a lovely setting for a picnic. This is a wonderful site for damsel and dragonflies and a great many species have been found here. A narrow path beside a sunken Norman trackway leads to the tiny village of Penrice where free range chickens sometimes scratch about on the green, enjoying their freedom: restrain little ones tempted to chase! Several points of historical interest include the church and the old castle ringwork. The steep winding lane leads back to the start. Only take children of an age and number who can be made to walk sensibly along the lane. Steep and winding, it has relatively little traffic, but motorists have restricted views on the bends. The road section can be shortened by not continuing to Penrice when the Norman trackway reaches the lane, or eliminated by simply retracing your steps back through the wood to the start.

Attractions
The Stew Ponds, probably constructed in 1785 are empty now. They were used to provide fresh fish for the Penrice Estate. A little further on are the ruins of a mill. A corn mill was built on this site in the sixteenth century but these remains probably date from 1785. It was in use until 1890. Two mill wheels can be seen there.

Spruce, oak, hazel and sycamore line the track to the lake and rhododendrons grow along the stream down to your left. The lake, with seats, is an ideal spot for a picnic. Get youngsters to notice the wildlife – in summer see how many different dragonflies and waterbirds there are, and look out for a robin perched on a branch nearby waiting for the crumbs to fall.

The sunken Norman trackway once linked Penrice and a hamlet at Capon's Hill. The twisted oaks growing on its banks are the remains of a pre-World War I oak wood. Near the top of the track on the left, but overgrown and not easily found, is the Penrice Well, used until 1948.

The quiet disposition of Penrice belies a past as the social and commercial centre of Gower. On the green is the base of a cross (absent since the eighteenth century), which became known as 'Crying Stone' because the auctioneer used to stand on it at the markets. The walls of the pound are still visible as you follow the road bearing right away from the village.

Continued on page 46

Route 9

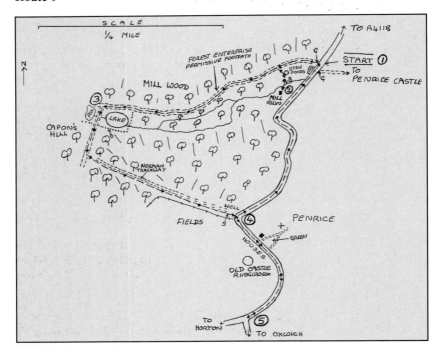

Penrice Green

44

Route 9
Mill Wood and Pennrice

$1\frac{1}{4}$ miles
(shorter variation $\frac{3}{4}$ mile)

Start

Penrice is situated just north of Oxwich. Take the southward turning signposted for Penrice from the A4118. After half a mile there is a small parking area on the right, opposite the gates of Penrice Estate (GR 493883).

1. *Enter Mill Wood through the gate above the car-park. The route from point 1 to point 3 is not along a right of way. This specially surfaced permissive footpath linking the car-park to the lakeside picnic area was constructed by the Forest Enterprise to enable use by people with walking difficulties and in wheelchairs. After about 100 yds, a few steps on the left go down to a track leading to a circular segmented stew pond. Follow the path to the right around it and cross the bridge over the stream to reach the mill ruin.*

2. *Retrace your steps to the main track and continue along it. You soon reach a lake.*

3. *From the far end of the lake turn left; on the right is a pool which flows into it. Take the narrow path up to the left shortly past the lake. Parallel to this on the left-hand side is a sunken Norman trackway. Near the top, tall larches are on the right, before it opens out to fields on that side.*

4. *Cross a stile and turn right at the road when you reach it. Continue with care along this narrow and steep lane to Penrice. You can find the church at the far end of the green. Continue along the road past the old walls of the pound and when it forks, turn round and look up to your left to see the old castle ringwork behind the village.*

5. *Retrace your steps back through Penrice and on down the road to the start.*

Shorter variation

As for 1 to 4 then; instead of turning right when you reach the road, to continue to Penrice, turn left and follow the road back to the start.

Public Transport

SWT provides a fairly regular service to Penrice. You would then start and finish the route at Penrice rather than at Mill Wood.

Penrice Church is dedicated to St Andrew. This twelfth century church is cruciform in shape, the unusually large porch corresponding with the north transept. The porch, which was added at a later date, would have been used for secular purposes. The inner door also has a peculiarity: unattached to the freestone jambs of the inner doorway, it is joined to an enormous oak frame and held against the freestone from inside by pillars of masonry. The restoration in 1894 discovered a small stone head of a female figure, possibly from an old tomb; it is now above the chancel arch. The outside walls of the north transept have blocked-up openings, possibly leading to an underground vault where members of the Penrice and Mansel families may have been buried. The font in this transept is Early English, but was probably later re-modelled. A single bell is enclosed in the embattled tower.

Penrice Old Castle is known as 'Mounty Bank'. The site of this early castle ringwork is now overgrown, but its size (the largest in Gower) and the height of its defensive banks suggest it was a major Gower castle. It was probably abandoned in the thirteenth century when the stone castle was erected nearby.

'Pennyhitch' is the name of the lane between the A4118 and the gates of Penrice Estate, so called because a horse was kept there to help heavy loads up the hill for a charge of one penny.

Refreshments
None. Take a picnic to have by the lake. The nearest shop and hotel are at Oxwich, a mile and a half along the road.

Lake in Mill Wood

46

Oxwich Bay and Nicholaston Wood

Outline
Oxwich Bay – Nicholaston Pill – Nicholaston Wood – Nicholaston Pill – Oxwich Bay

Summary
Centred in a National Nature Reserve, this walk combines a breezy stroll along the sweeping Oxwich Bay which children love, followed by airy, sun-splashed tracks through Nicholaston Wood. There are fine views over the varied habitats of the reserve. With quietness, many seashore and woodland birds may be seen. The reserve centre in the car-park is well worth a visit.

At peak times during the high season the beach can become exhaustingly crowded and noisy; otherwise it is usually quiet, and even empty. Although a longer ramble, it is relatively easy with wide woodland tracks, except for one stretch which is stony and uneven. You are quite close to the road at one point; in an emergency someone could fetch the car.

Attractions
This National Nature Reserve is particularly interesting as it has an unusually wide variety of habitats, harbouring many species of wildlife. Look along the shoreline of Oxwich Bay for sea potato, sponges, and in summer, the huge jellyfish, *Rhizostoma Octopus*. Razor shells are especially common. Gulls and oystercatchers are invariably present and other possibilities include cormorant, gannet, sandpiper, redshank and, in winter, sanderling. Little ones can count the different types of seaweed and shells in the sand. Damaged during World War II the dunes, although unstable, have recovered, and now a tremendous variety of plants and insects inhabit them.

Nicholaston Pill is a popular haunt for shore birds and waders. Look in the water for shoals of small fish. As you view Nicholaston Wood from the Pill, Crawley Wood is further east along the slope with its prominent limestone outcrop, Crawley Bluff, which was once quarried.

Ash and sycamore predominate in Nicholaston Wood but there are also spruce, fir and rhododendron. Look out for buzzard, kestrel, tawny owl, sparrowhawk and woodpecker. After a climb you see the marsh and sluice down to your left. At point 4 you are quite close to the road to Oxwich. In an emergency (do not attempt this otherwise as the road can be extremely busy) take the single path onwards, instead of the wide track from the right. This leads to the road where you can wait while someone turns left down the road and walks for over a mile to fetch the car.

In the upper part of the wood oaks are more common. You will pass the viewpoint from where you can see the freshwater and saltmarshes, Nicholaston Pill, the dunes, Oxwich Bay and Point and the village itself.

Continued on page 50

Route 10

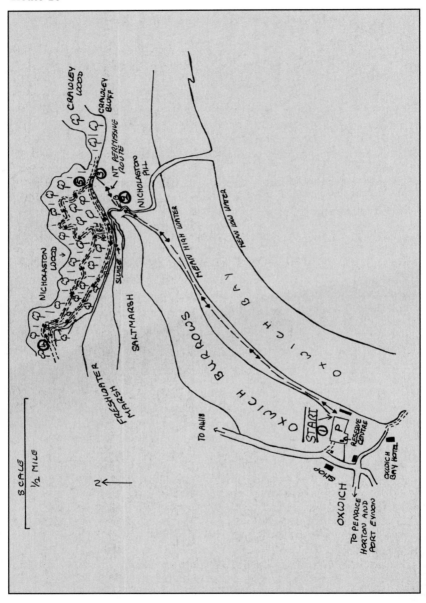

Route 10
Oxwich Bay and Nicholaston Wood

$4\frac{1}{2}$ miles

Start

Oxwich is situated on the south Gower coast. Take the Oxwich turning south from the A4118. Park in the large car-park on the Marsh Road (GR 502865).

1. *Turn left out of the car-park and walk along the long stretch of beach to Nicholaston Pill. Here, the Oxwich dunes cease. Turn left alongside the Pill and cross it via the bridge.*

2. *To your left is a wooded slope with some areas of bare rock face showing. You are heading to the first lowest rock in the trees: this is the entrance to the woodland track. Make your way to this point via one of the many paths over the flattish area of Nicholaston Burrows ahead of you. This is a National Trust permissive route over Nicholaston Burrows.*

3. *Take the path leading to the left up into the woodland past a sign for the Oxwich National Nature Reserve. Once in the woodland the path forks; go left along the lower edge of the wood, then follow the path as it climbs. Continue along this track until it is eventually joined by another wide track from the right.*

4. *Turn up on to this (ignoring the single track onwards), for a return through the upper part of the wood. Past the viewpoint, the track becomes darker as it bends away from the edge; descending slightly, it becomes stony and uneven. After a slight climb the track curves to the right, descending steeply in places, towards the marsh.*

5. *You will meet the lower path which you initially took into the wood; turn left and exit past the reserve sign. From here, retrace your steps along the beach to the start.*

Public Transport
SWT provides a fairly regular service to Oxwich.

The Freshwater Marsh and Saltmarshes are seen on this walk from Nicholaston Wood; the freshwater marsh behind the sluice used to be saltmarsh, but at the end of the eighteenth century the sluice was built to stop seawater flooding the area, and it became good grazing land. However, earlier this century it 'degraded' into a freshwater marsh. The saltmarsh floods in high spring tides. Look out for herons over this area.

Refreshments
A shop is opposite the car-park and shops open in the holiday season edge the bay. The Oxwich Bay Hotel welcomes children and high chairs are available. There is a large garden overlooking the bay.

Oxwich Castle

Oxwich Point

Outline
Oxwich – Oxwich Wood – Oxwich Point – Oxwich Castle – Oxwich

Summary
This route runs past the tiny, hidden Oxwich Church; then after ascending about 200 steep steps, it continues along the twisting paths of Oxwich Wood, part of a National Nature Reserve.

Descending more steps towards the sea you round the open headland of Oxwich Point; views on a clear day extend across the shimmering channel to the North Devon and Somerset coastline, and to Lundy Island. The route then turns inland, across farmland to the enormous Oxwich Castle ruins, before descending a stretch of road into the village.

In view of the steps and the very narrow path through gorse round Oxwich Point this route may not be suited to very young children.

Attractions
The small Oxwich Church, dedicated to St Illtyd, is probably twelfth century, but stands on ground made sacred well before that. The embattled tower, however, is thirteenth or fourteenth century and its single bell, inscribed 'Sancta Maria ora pro nobis' – St Mary pray for us – is nearly, if not as old. The chancel, said to be a Celtic cell, is the smallest in Gower. In the churchyard lies a dried up well which was said to be haunted. The steps ascending from the church are a long, steep climb.

Oxwich Wood forms part of a National Nature Reserve. Here, the trees are highly unusual: principally oak and ash, they are conspicuously low-growing and stunted due to wind pruning.

With rock pools down to your left, the wood is replaced by the gorse-covered slopes of Oxwich Point. Here the path is very narrow. Look back to view Cefn Bryn across the bay, and east along the coastline to Pwlldu Head and Whiteshell Point.

The impressive ruins of Oxwich Castle are all that remains of a large mansion house, built by the Mansel family in the sixteenth century, out of the original castle belonging to them. The smaller ruin beside the castle is a stone pigeon house. Over the entrance, between two towers, is carved the Mansel family crest.

Care of traffic needs to be taken when returning along the road towards Oxwich and in the village itself as it can be busy. Oxwich was a poor village where agricultural labouring was supplemented, among other things, by smuggling and wrecking. In the early nineteenth century, the cliffs of Oxwich Point were quarried for limestone which was exported from the small port to Devon. Many traditional Gower cottages remain in the village, one of which, now 'Nook Cottage', was used by John Wesley during the eighteenth century. The reserve centre in the car-park is well worth a visit.

Route 11

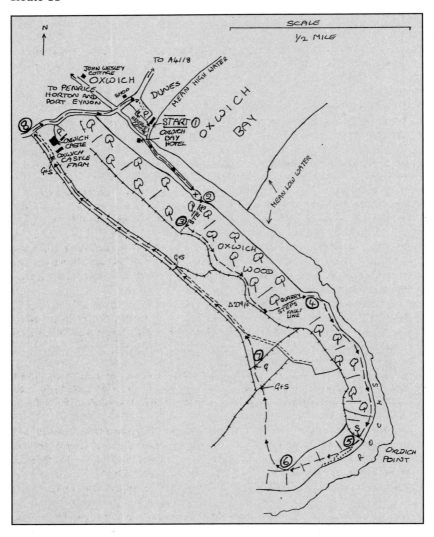

Route 11
Oxwich Point

$3\frac{1}{4}$ miles

Start

Situated on the south Gower coast, Oxwich is reached by taking the turning south, signposted for Oxwich, from the A4118. Park in the large car-park on the Marsh Road (GR 502865).

1. *From the car-park turn right on to the beach and walk towards the Oxwich Bay Hotel. Turn left into the narrow road, and follow it beside the bay to St Illtyd's Church.*

2. *Just past the church, take the steps up to the right.*

3. *Near the top take the clear path which leads off to the left, winding through low-growing trees. Remain on this path as it continues near the edge of the woodland beside a fence, before bearing left down steps and descending towards the sea.*

4. *You come out of the woodland along the cliff edge with rocks and rock pools down to the left. Follow the path, in and out of small oaks until the wood gives way to gorse-covered slopes on your right. This is Oxwich Point. Continue past firebeaters and a reserve sign, then cross a stile.*

5. *A few yards past the stile, the narrow path forks, left to Port Eynon, and right to Oxwich Green. Take the upper right-hand path. Go right again at a second fork to climb steadily up the slope.*

6. *At the top is a signpost for Oxwich Green pointing straight over the gorse-invaded field. Follow this with gorse on your right, to a waymarked gate and stile in the wall. Cross the stile and a small field to another waymarked gate on the other side.*

7. *Go through this into the next field and turn left along the hard track running through it. The trig point of 279 ft is on your right where the scrub ends. Soon you meet a gate and stile which you cross, entering a hedge-bordered lane. Exit the lane where it ends, by crossing the stile beside a gate. Oxwich Castle Farm is on your right. Walk ahead down the stony drive past Oxwich Castle on the right.*

8. *Turn right onto the tarmac road, and walk with care down to the village. Turn left at the crossroads if you wish to visit the John Wesley Cottage, which is on the right about 100 yards along the road. Otherwise, cross straight over to reach the car-park on the right.*

Public Transport

SWT operates a fairly regular service to Oxwich.

Refreshments
A shop is opposite the car-park and shops open in the holiday season edge the bay.
The Oxwich Bay Hotel welcomes children and high chairs are available. There is a
large garden overlooking the bay.

Rhossili

Rhossili Vile

Outline

Rhossili – Rhossili Vile – Worm's Head – Rhossili

Summary

A refreshing, short and easy walk through Rhossili Vile, where the ancient pattern of medieval open field cultivation can still be seen. The route, entering a National Nature Reserve, then turns to the open, blowy headland above Worm's Head, the most westerly tip of the peninsula. The spectacular coastal scenery continues, as turning towards Rhossili is a view of the wide, sweeping bay overshadowed by the dramatic, often mist-clad Rhossili Down.

Providing tide times are checked there is the possibility of extending the walk, to the rock pools on the causeway below, and for sure-footed, active family members to scramble out on to the serpent-like 'Worm' itself.

Attractions

Rhossili is the most westerly of the Gower villages; windswept and treeless, the area is open to Atlantic gales and wild seas. In the past a strong Methodist tradition reigned, and the principal occupation was agriculture. An ideal position for smuggling, the industry became powerful in the eighteenth and early nineteenth centuries. Goods from wrecks and wrecking also aided a meagre living. During the nineteenth century the cliffs were quarried heavily and the limestone exported by sea, from 'Flotquars' (floating quarries), to Devon.

Rhossili Church, dedicated to St Mary the Virgin, was probably built in the thirteenth century. Its principal ornate attraction is the arch over the doorway which has intricate dog-tooth and chevron carving. The arch is a rare example of twelfth century workmanship, and it is said to have been transported up from an earlier besanded church in the Warren (see Rhossili Bay; route 13).

Rhossili Vile is an unusual site, where the pattern of medieval open field cultivation remains clear. The field would be divided into many strips with low grass banks, 'landshares', between them. People would cultivate strips in different parts of the area, the aim being to share out fairly the good and poor land. Corn and, because of the relatively frost-free climate, root vegetables, did especially well. In the last century, common rights allowed everyone to graze their animals on the land, just after the harvest. Now, although there are fewer farmers, market gardening is still continued today. Notice the slanting hawthorns shaped by the strong westerly winds.

From the Vile the route takes you to the old coastguard lookout, now the reserve centre and worth a visit. Look out for oystercatchers and turnstones on the causeway at low tide. On a clear day the North Devon and Somerset coastline, and Lundy Island are visible across the Bristol Channel.

Continued on page 58

Route 12

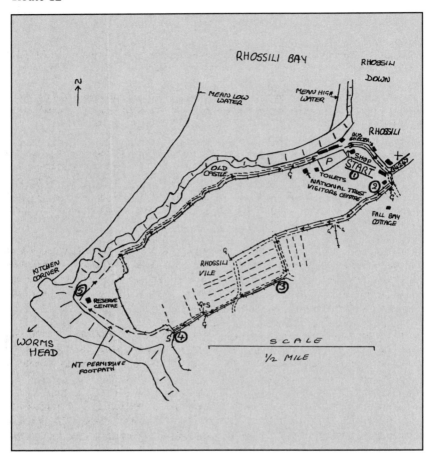

Route 12
Rhossili Vile   **2 miles**

Start

Situated on the west coast, Rhossili is at the end of the B4247. Turn off the A4118 at Scurlage, and park in Rhossili car-park at the end of the road (GR 415881).

1. *Walk with care back up the road from the car-park, and at the first left-hand bend (just before the church, which you can visit) take the lane which leads off to the right.*

2. *From here, take the first turning to the right, where there is a gate and inconspicuous sign for 'Fall Bay Cottage'. Continue straight down as a fence replaces the hedge on the right and low banks replace the one on the left. Ahead, and to the left, are the open fields of the Vile. The track forks; straight on towards a gate and sharply left where it continues between open fields. Go left and follow it as it bends again, now to the right.*

3. *Continue down the wide, grassy track with a low hedge on the left and open field cultivation on the right. Go straight over when a second wide track crosses at an angle. When the track bends to the right in front of a gate, then immediately bends to the left, stay with it and, after the second bend, cross the bar stile beside a gate. Continue down towards the coast.*

4. *Cross the bar stile ahead, which leads out on to the cliffs. Turn right along the path to the reserve centre on the cliff above Worm's Head. This part of the route, as you walk along the top of the cliffs above Worm's Head to the reserve centre, is along a National Trust permissive footpath.*

5. *Turn right down the wide grass walk, then take the gravel track, a bridleway, beside a wall on the right. Stay on this track, avoiding the tempting grassy cliffs which have dangerous steep slopes to the sea. Go through the gate at the end to the car-park ahead of you.*

Public Transport

SWT provides a fairly regular service to Rhossili.

Worm's Head is a mile-long tidal island. 'Worm', in Old English, meant serpent or dragon. It is formed of limestone and the three humps are known as the Inner, Middle and Outer Heads. 'Devil's Bridge' links the Middle and Outer Heads, while the latter contains two interesting features. The first is the blow hole, a cleft in the rock through which air, and in heavy seas, sprays of water, are forced. The second is Worm's Head Cave, situated at the furthest tip. Bones of rhinoceros, mammoth and bear have been excavated, and a legend existed of an underground passage linking this cave with a cave at the head of Gwendraeth Fach in Carmarthenshire. The Inner Head once supported an Iron Age fort. It is good, if impractical, agricultural land, and sheep still graze there in the winter. The 'Worm' is also an attractive place for sea birds, and houses important breeding colonies of razorbills, guillemots and kittiwakes. For this reason visitors are asked not to go on to the Outer Head during the breeding season, which is from 1st March to 15th August.

If you wish to visit the 'Worm', ensure you check the tide times first as it is easy to get cut off by the rising tide (the reserve centre and National Trust visitor centre both give this information). The causeway is open for about $2\frac{1}{2}$ hours either side of low water. Please keep to the footpath as the grasslands are of an ancient and fragile form.

The route turns towards Rhossili. During summer, stonechats and yellowhammers can frequently be seen flitting about in the gorse. The cliffs along here have been quarried heavily and notice, on the same side, Old Castle fort, the site of a much-damaged Iron Age promontory fort.

Refreshments
The Worm's Head Hotel admits children, and there is a terrace for customers. There are several tea rooms situated near the car-park.

Worm's Head from Rhossili Bay

Rhossili Down

Outline
Rhossili – Rhossili Down – Hillend – Rhossili Bay – Rhossili

Summary
Rhossili Down is frequently mist-enshrouded, hiding its crags and 'wild' ponies; yet on a clear day, this ridge with its summit the highest point in Gower, yields far-reaching views from Devon to Pembrokeshire, and still retains a feel of remoteness. My favourite walk, it is at its best in August when blanketed by deep purple heather, with swallows skimming low, hunting the countless insects. The return can be along the base of the down, past the Old Rectory, or alternatively, along the wide, golden sands of Rhossili Bay.

Generally an easy walk, it does, however, have a steep climb and descent. It tends to feel longer than the mileage suggests! With a road at Hillend, it is possible for someone to fetch the car, if necessary.

Attractions
For details of Rhossili Church and Rhossili village see Route 12. Both Rhossili Down and Rhossili Bay are National Trust properties.

Rhossili Down is formed of Old Red Sandstone. This ridge contains the highest point in Gower, 633 ft. As you climb to the ridge look back to see Rhossili and Middleton, and beyond, to the ancient field pattern of Rhossili Vile, the Worm's Head and the South Gower coast. On a clear day, Lundy Island and the cliffs of the North Devon and Somerset coast are visible. As you reach the ridge, the gorse gives way entirely to heather. Ahead, you can see the beacon indicating the highest point.

Look out for flattened cairns as the path undulates along the top of the down. About 14 Bronze Age cairns can be found on the down. They are single burial tombs built by primitive agriculturalists around 2000 BC. The summit beacon is sited on one of these cairns.

As you continue, down to your right, although not visible from here, are two Sweyne Howes. These are Megalithic chambered tombs, built over 4000 years ago. Traditionally this is said to be the place where Sweyne, a Viking warrior, was buried. Similar tombs include Parc le Breos chambered tomb and Arthur's Stone. From here you can return via the sweeping Rhossili Bay or along the cliffs at the base of the down.

Rhossili Bay, a wide, three mile sweep of golden sand edged by the white surf of the Atlantic waves, is not only beautiful, but is of historical interest too. Near Rhossili, between the down and the beach, a sloping area of bracken-covered dunes, known as the Warren, conceals a buried village, possibly of pre-Norman Conquest times. The remains of a church, graveyard and other buildings have been excavated

Continued on page 62

Route 13

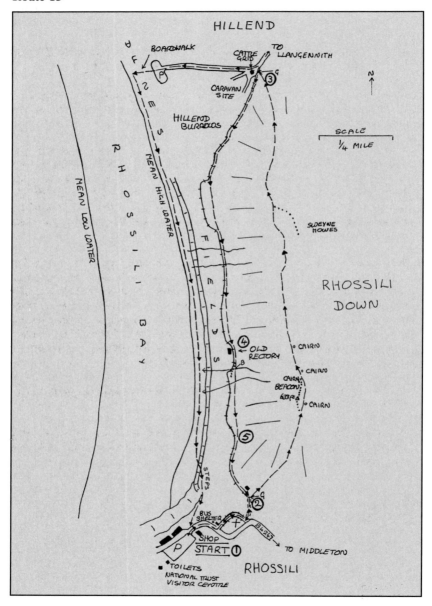

Route 13
Rhossili Down   **4 miles**

Start
Situated on the west coast, Rhossili is at the end of the B4247. Turn off the A4118 at
Scurlage. Park in Rhossili car-park at the end of the road (GR 415881).

1. *Walk back up the road from the car-park. At the bus shelter take the path off to the*
   left; it runs behind the church, which is well worth a visit. From here, turn left
   towards the base of the down.

2. *Pass a signpost for Rhossili Bay, and a little further on go through a kissing-gate.*
   Now take the right-hand path, a bridleway, which leads over the top of the down to
   Hillend. Remain on this wide track, climbing steeply through gorse and heather.
   Follow the ridge, passing the beacon indicating the highest point to your left. The
   path undulates along the top of the down until, at the north end, with Hillend and
   Broughton Bay in view, it descends from the ridge to the Hillend caravan site. Walk
   with care down this steep path.

3. *On reaching the gate at the bottom, you can return via the beach or along the cliffs*
   at the base of the down. For the beach, go through the gate, and enter the caravan
   site over a cattle grid at the further of the two entrances on your left. Take the lower
   right-hand fork and follow it to where it ends in a car-park. From here, take the
   boardwalk through the dunes to the beach. Turn left, and continue along the sand,
   until below Rhossili you find steps leading up to the village. Alternatively, to return
   along the bridleway at the base of the down, do not go through the gate, but take the
   lower left-hand path beside the caravan site and fence.

4. *Continue until you reach the Old Rectory. Here, take the upper path to the left,*
   which crosses a bridge after a short distance.

5. *Walking beside a wall again, you will see Rhossili village ahead. Follow the path,*
   passing buildings on the left, and you will reach the kissing-gate through which you
   came earlier. From here, retrace your steps to the start.

Public Transport
SWT operates a fairly regular service to Rhossili.

61

along with some pottery. It was besanded, probably in the fourteenth century, as were the churches of Penmaen and Pennard.

There are remains of at least three wrecks visible along Rhossili sands. The *Verani*, was wrecked in 1894 beneath the Old Castle cliffs at the southern end. At low tide the skeleton of the bows belonging to the *Helvetia* are conspicuous near Rhossili; she was blown on to the sands in 1887. Near Hillend at very low tides, the remains of a paddle-steamer, the *City of Bristol*, wrecked here in 1840, can still be seen. A Spanish galleon wrecked here in the seventeenth century shed her cargo of Spanish silver dollars. A quantity have since been recovered, and a tale exists claiming that a member of the Mansel family of Old Henllys, made off with much of the cargo, and some say that his coach and four grey horses haunt the bay.

Whatever happened, it is generally considered that buried treasure still lies beneath Rhossili sands.

If you choose to return along the base of the down look out for kestrels hovering above the dunes. You will pass the Old Rectory, the site of which is ancient, possibly monastic, although the rectory itself (said to be haunted) was rebuilt in the middle of the last century. It is now a holiday home. Near the Rectory, a successful hide-out for smuggled goods was constructed under the stream bed. It has since collapsed. Further along you can see, on the sands at low tide, the remains of the *Helvetia*.

Refreshments
The Worm's Head Hotel admits children, there is a terrace for customers. There are several tea rooms situated near the car-park.

Rhossili Bay

Hardings Down

Outline

Llangennith Road – Upper Hardingsdown – Hardings Down – Iron Age Fort – Upper Hardingsdown – Llangennith Road

Summary

This walk, which is situated off the main road, is quieter than other heathland routes, while still enjoying extensive and ever-changing views as the hill is circled. 'Wild' ponies and sheep now graze on the down which has sites of three Iron Age forts. It is a short, easy walk, and being largely along a stone track it makes a good winter stroll.

Attractions

Reaching 500 feet, Hardings Down is the smallest of the three hills in West Gower which are formed of Old Red Sandstone, the other two being Rhossili Down and Llanmadoc Hill.

As you start to circle the hill Ryer's Down and Cefn Bryn are the two main hills visible; between them you can see deep into east Gower. On reaching the far side, the formidable rise of Rhossili Down looms ahead. As you begin to face north-west, Llangennith and Broughton Burrows, and the tidal island, Burry Holms, all come into view. From the fort Llanmadoc Hill is out to the left, and the sea beyond Broughton Bay is visible, edged by the dark line of the South Wales coast. There is a small site of an Iron Age fort on the north side of the hill and one on the summit, while the largest is on the west side. It had banks, a ditch and ramparts for defences. As just three hut sites have been excavated, it seems likely that this was one of the forts inhabited only in troubled times.

Refreshments

The nearest are at The Kings Head Hotel in Llangennith where there is also a shop.

Route 14

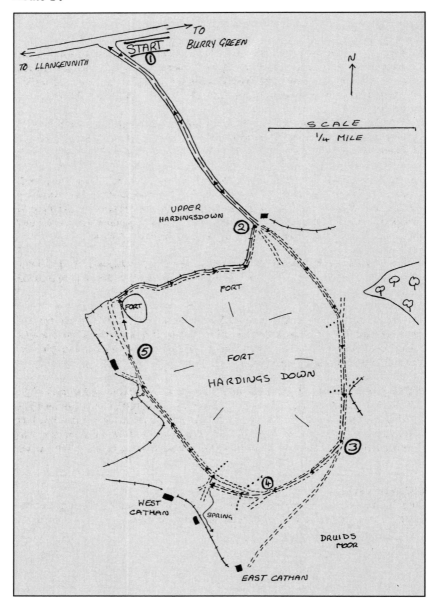

Route 14
Hardings Down

$2\frac{1}{4}$ miles

Start

Hardings Down is situated south-east of Llangennith. From Burry Green take the road towards Llangennith; after passing a right-hand turn for Llanmadoc, the road climbs. The left-hand turning for Hardings Down is just after the brow of the hill as you begin to descend towards Llangennith; this is the start (GR 433915).

1. *Walk along the road approaching Hardings Down. The tarmac gives way to a stony farm road, but continue until you reach the base of the down. The rest of the route follows a bridleway.*

2. *Here, three main tracks face you; the stony farm road continues ahead, then bends sharply right. To the left is a wide grass track, which forks off the farm road and leads through bracken. Take this track, not the narrower one just to the right of it. Remain on this track, which can be muddy and wet, ignoring others which cross and join it. Fairly soon you join a stony farm road, turn right along it.*

3. *On the far side the track forks where, low to the ground and pointing to the right-hand fork, is a sign for Whitemoor. Take this right-hand fork, keeping tight to the hill.*

4. *When the track next forks go right. Then very shortly it forks again, the two resulting tracks continuing almost parallel. The right of way runs along the left-hand fork which gives way to grass, before crossing over to the right-hand fork, in order to continue circling the down.*

5. *Having rejoined the stony farm road, continue, and you pass a farm to the left. Here, the right of way again temporarily leaves the road, cutting across to the right and passing the site of the large hill fort, before it rejoins the farm road, which is now beside a fence. Eventually the farm road bends sharply left, returning you to the original point at the base of the down. From here retrace your steps to the start.*

Public Transport

A highly infrequent bus service does operate to Llangennith but it is geared to people making a day-trip from the village rather than to it.

Hang-gliding and para-gliding from Rhossili Down

Ryer's Down and Burry Pill

Outline
Ryer's Down – Burry Pill – Stembridge – Western Mill – Ryer's Down

Summary
A pretty walk combining the open Ryer's Down with paths through woodland and valley. A moss-strewn sunken lane leads through the rich, green and brown glory of beech woods, to the clear, gurgling Burry Pill, a huge attraction for little ones. The path remains near the stream as the route continues through fields, with lots of stiles to cross! The return is along the base of the down where 'wild' ponies and sheep graze.

The walk is not difficult but entails a steep descent. Where you meet a road at Stembridge, it would be possible for someone to fetch the car, if necessary.

Attractions
With the first climb you are rewarded with a view, in clear conditions, of north Gower, Llanelli on the far side of the estuary, and further to the Brecon Beacons. Descending to the base of the down it can be quite slippery. In the sunken lane take time to notice the moss along its sides and to contemplate the majesty of the beech woodland.

You hear running water, and shortly you reach the Burry Pill. It is a delightful stream, which once powered six mills on its way to the Burry Estuary, where it flows over the marsh into the Loughor Estuary and the sea.

The route takes you in the other direction, up-stream towards Stembridge Mill. Now a private house undergoing renovation, it used to be one of the nineteenth century woollen mills.

The final section takes you along the bridleway at the base of Ryer's Down from where you retrace your steps to the start.

Refreshments
None here, take a picnic! However, the Britannia Inn is situated at a junction three-quarters of a mile further along the road towards Cheriton.

Route 15

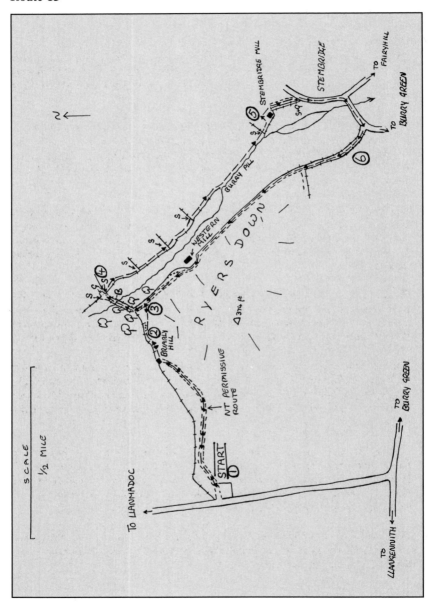

Route 15
Ryer's Down and Burry Pill

3 miles

Start

Ryer's Down is situated just north of Burry Green. From here, follow the Llangennith road, and then take the right-hand turning signposted for Llanmadoc. The walk begins half a mile along the road, where a stony track leads off to the right (GR 449922).

1. *Walk up the stony road towards the down. This is not a right of way but it is a National Trust permissive route. Where it stops just past a house on your left, continue ahead and take the narrow, grassy path through bracken, beside a fence on the left. After a climb the path then descends through bracken, and a few birch, oak and rowan.*

2. *Near the base of the hill the path forks slightly; take the upper, right-hand fork, which leads through hazel, before emerging into the open again with a telegraph pole just ahead. Bear right with the path, and head for a single ash tree some yards to the right of the others. Here, the path continues bending, now with the wood on the left.*

3. *Continue; by an oak tree, the path turns sharply down to the left, and after a few yards you meet the bridleway which runs along the base of the down. Turn left, towards the woodland. Where the track forks, bear right down the sunken lane through mainly beech woodland. You cross a stone bridge over the Burry Pill.*

4. *Once over the bridge you are faced with two stiles; cross the right-hand one into a field. Turn right, and walk along the valley at the base of the fields. Keep beside the hedge/fence on your right, and cross stiles as you meet them. The Burry Pill is over to the right, but after the third stile a small field comes between your path and the stream.*

5. *After a final stile, you reach Stembridge Mill. Take the path to the left of it, then turn on to the stony drive and walk down its short distance to a gate and stile which lead into the road. Cross the stile, turn right and walk with care down the road. You cross the Burry Pill, and as the road begins to climb, take the stony lane, a bridleway, off to the right (beside the remains of a signpost).*

6. *Continue along the bridleway at the base of the down, past Western Mill and on to the place where you joined it at point 3. From here retrace your steps over the side of the down and back to the start.*

Public Transport
There is no bus service to the start of this route.

Arthur's Stone

Arthur's Stone

Outline
Road crossing Cefn Bryn – Arthur's Stone – Cairn – Road crossing Cefn Bryn

Summary
A short, easy, circular walk on top of Cefn Bryn passing Gower's prime historical monument, Arthur's Stone. Views extend over North Gower, and on a clear day to Pembrokeshire and the Brecon Beacons. It has the advantage of being quieter than the main track which leads directly to Arthur's Stone, and is just as easy.

Attractions
Cefn Bryn is the Old Red Sandstone 'backbone' of Gower. Common land, it is grazed by 'wild' ponies and sheep.

As you walk from the road towards Arthur's Stone, at the base of Cefn Bryn you can see Broad Pool, a reserve of the Glamorgan Wildlife Trust, which is excellent for botanists. Beyond Llanrhidian, at low tide the network of streams flowing over the saltmarsh is visible, and further west, Whiteford Sands jut out into the estuary. On a clear day, north-east of the estuary the Brecon Beacons are visible, and to the north-west are Pembrokeshire's Presceli Hills.

King Arthur's Stone or 'Maen Cetti' is a magnificent reminder of prehistoric man. It is a Neolithic tomb with two burial chambers, built by primitive agriculturalists around 2500 BC. A huge glacial boulder weighing over 25 tons serves as the capstone. It is surrounded by the remains of a cairn and may have been buried completely at one time. The capstone has been the subject of many legends including one that claims it was a pebble King Arthur found in his shoe, and another, which tells how it was split by his sword, 'Excalibur'.

Facing westwards the hills are: Rhossili Down, Hardings Down, Ryer's Down and Llanmadoc Hill. The cairn which you pass is just one of over 60 cairns built around 3000–2000 BC, which have been found on Cefn Bryn, although most are obscured by summer vegetation.

Refreshments
None! Although you may find an ice cream van here in peak season.

Route 16

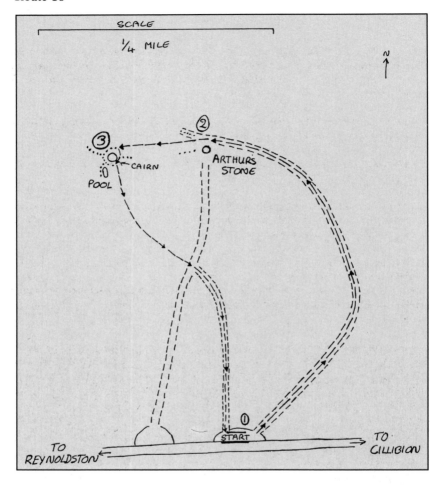

Route 16
Arthur's Stone

1 mile

Start

> Take the only road which crosses Cefn Bryn, linking Reynoldston in the south and Cillibion in North Gower. On the ridge is a large, clear area and a little further east along the road on the north side, is a second clear area. This is the start (GR 493900).

1. *From the clear area take the wide, grassy track out to the right, heading just to the right of the rise ahead of you. Follow the track as it bears left.*

2. *On reaching Arthur's Stone, the track forks; take the left-hand path, which shortly leads to a cairn. Close to it is a pool.*

3. *From here take the second path to your left, heading back towards the start. Cross straight over the main track leading to Arthur's Stone and soon you will reach the clear area where you began.*

Public Transport

SWT provides a fairly regular service to Reynoldston Green. From there you could walk along the road up to Cefn Bryn ridge.

The view south from the base of Cefn Bryn

73

Path from Bishopston Church (Route 1)

Useful information

Walks in order of difficulty
An experienced walker would not class any of these walks as difficult. In the context of a Family Walks guide this grading has been made with a fairly active 7 or 8 year old in mind.

Easy Walks:
Route 4 *West Cliff and Pennard Castle.*
Route 5 *Ilston Cwm.*
Route 7 *Cefn Bryn.*
Route 9 *Mill Wood and Penrice.*
Route 10 *Oxwich Bay and Nicholaston Wood.*
Route 12 *Rhossili Vile.*
Route 14 *Hardings Down.*
Route 15 *Ryer's Down and Burry Pill.*
Route 16 *Arthur's Stone.*

Moderately Difficult:
Route 2 *Brandy Cove and Lower Bishopston Valley.*
Route 3 *Pwlldu Head and Lower Bishopston Valley.*
Route 6 *Park Woods and Green Cwm.*
Route 8 *Penmaen Burrows.*
Route 11 *Oxwich Point.*
Route 13 *Rhossili Down.*

More Strenuous:
Route 1 *Bishopston Valley.*

Bus Operators
Gower – The South Wales Transport Co, Ltd (SWT). (0792) 582233
Some other companies operating in the area
D Coaches (0792) 791981
Rees and Williams (0269) 592680
Silverline Quality Small Coaches (0685) 382406
Red and White (0633) 265100
Cardiff Buses (0222) 396521
Brewers Motor Ltd. (0656) 647093

Tourist Information Centres
Civic Information Centre, Swansea (0792) 468321
Information Centre, Oystermouth (0792) 361302
Wales Tourist Board (0222) 499909
Cardiff Tourist Information Centre (0222) 227281
Port Talbot Information Centre (0639) 823049
Caerleon Tourist Information Centre (0633) 430777

Other Places of Interest

I have listed some of the places to visit in Gower and over a wide area. There are still many more places not mentioned here of which details can be obtained from the Tourist Information Office. Opening times may change and hours are not given here. Telephone first before embarking on a journey.

Gower: Small World Pony Centre, Old Walls, Llanrhidian (0792) 390995. Open daily Apr–Oct. Rare miniature ponies – other animals – play areas.

Gower: Gower Farm Museum, Llandewi, Reynoldston (0792) 319247/391195. Open daily 10–5 Apr–Oct. Rare breeds – animals and birds – play and picnic areas.

Carmarthen: Gwili Steam Railway, Bronwydd (0267) 230666. Trips along Gwili valley – riverside picnic area. Telephone for open times.

Llanelli: The Wildfowl and Wetlands Trust, Penclawydd, Llwynhendy (0554) 741087. Open daily. Captive wildfowl – wild birds – hides – exhibitions – shop.

Neath: Aberdulais Falls, Aberdulais National Trust (0639) 636674. Open summer Apr–Oct, winter Nov and part of Dec. Famous waterfall – unique hydro-electric scheme.

Neath: Neath Canal Start at Resolven Basin (0639) 641121. About 4 miles – towpath walk – boat trips – aqueducts – bridges.

Country Parks

Swansea Valley: Craig-y-Nos Country Park, Pen-y-Cae (0639) 730395. Park open daily, Visitor centre Easter–Oct daily – riverside, meadow and woodland walks.

Bridgend: Bryngarw Country Park (0656) 725155. Visitor centre – playground – Japanese garden – lake – woodland and riverside walks.

Llandeilo: Gelli Aur Country Park, Golden Grove (0558) 668885. Open daily. Visitor centre – playground – deer park – gardens – arboretum – parkland – guided walks – nature trail.

Pembrey: Pembrey Country Park (0554) 833913. Open daily. Visitor centre – play area – nature trails – beach – railway – dry ski – putt golf – equestrian centre – restaurant.

Port Talbot: Margam Park (0639) 881635. Open Apr–Sept daily, Oct–Mar Wed–Sun. Attractions not running during winter. Fairytale Land – deer herd – castle – road train – maze – putting – audio-visual theatre.

Nature Trails

Gower: Bishops Wood, Caswell Bay (0792) 361703/302749. Open daily, Countryside Centre Apr–Sept most weekends and Bank holidays. Limestone grassland, scrub and woodland – 46 acres.

Tondu: Glamorgan Nature Centre, Park Pond Nature Reserve (0656) 724100. Open Mon–Fri. Small display area.

Wet Weather Alternatives

Completely or partly under cover.

Museums

Swansea: Swansea Museum (0792) 653763. Open daily except Mondays. Natural history displays, including Gower wildlife – pottery – archaeology – Egyptian priest mummy – costume – domestic artifacts.

Swansea: Maritime and Industrial Museum (0792) 650351/470371. Open daily except Mondays. Working woollen mill – transport and tramshed displays – floating exhibits.

Cardiff: The National Museum of Wales (0222) 397951. Open daily except Mondays. Welsh and International art – natural history – geology – archaeology – sculpture.

Cardiff: Welsh Industrial and Maritime Museum (0222) 481919. Open daily except Mondays. Evolution of Welsh road, rail and sea transport.

Llandysul: Museum of the Welsh Woollen Industry, Dre-fach, Felindre (0559) 370929. Open Apr–Sept Mon–Sat, Oct–Mar Mon–Fri. Production of woollen cloth – history of the industry.

Neath: Neath Museum (0639) 645741. Open Tue–Sat. Small museum – local history.

Neath: Cefn Coed Colliery Museum, Crynant (0639) 750556. Open daily. Coalmining – site of former colliery.

Galleries

Swansea: Swansea Arts Workshop Gallery (0792) 652016. Open Tue–Sun. Art – craft –design.

Swansea: Attic Gallery (0792) 653387. Open daily except Sundays. Sculpture – paintings and prints – local and contemporary.

Swansea: Glynn Vivian Art Gallery (0792) 655006. Open Tue–Sun. Paintings – Swansea ceramics – clocks – glass – exhibitions – shop.

Swansea: The Ocean Gallery, Sea Front Promenade (0792) 648180. Open daily. Sales – jewellery – ceramics – paintings – prints.

Oystermouth: The Lovespoon Gallery (0792) 360132. Open Mon–Sat. First gallery just for Lovespoons.

Crafts

Swansea: The Craft Workshops and Pottery (0792) 653871. Open Mon–Fri. Various crafts people at work – 12 studios – sales.

Upper Swansea Valley: The Coach House, Craig-y-Nos (0639) 730767. Open summer daily, winter Wed–Sun. Craft shop – licenced restaurant – food all day.

Llandeilo: Trapp Arts and Crafts Centre, Trapp (0269) 850362. Open Mar–Christmas daily except Mondays. Art gallery – craft sales – demonstrations – exhibitions – tea room.

Ryer's Down (Route 15)

Historic Buildings

A few historic buildings while worth visiting in wet weather, are perhaps more suited to dryer conditions. Telephone to check before visiting.

Gower: Woebley Castle, Llanrhidian (0792) 390012. Open daily. Thirteenth century fortified manor house – exhibition on the castle's history and Gower.

Oystermouth: Oystermouth Castle (0792) 302727. Open daily Apr–Oct. Norman castle – dramatic setting.

Cardiff: Cardiff Castle (0222) 822083. Open daily. Roman fort with Norman and Medieval remains – lodgings largely nineteenth century – guided tours.

Kidwelly: Kidwelly Castle (0554) 890104. Open daily. Late thirteenth century castle – well preserved – sited at estuary of the Gwendraeth fach – footpaths – shop.

Neath: Neath Abbey (0792) 812387. Open daily. Cistercian Abbey – fairly complete ruins.

Newport: Caerleon Roman Fortress, Caerleon (0633) 422518. Fortress AD75 – fortress baths – barracks – amphitheatre.

Various

Swansea: Swansea Leisure Centre (0792) 649126. Open daily.

Swansea: Plantasia (0792) 474555. Open daily except Mondays. Tropical, desert and humid zones – 5000 plants – aviary – reptile centre – butterfly house.

Upper Swansea Valley: Dan-Yr-Ogof Show Caves, Glyntawe, Abercraf (0639) 730284. Open Apr–Oct. Largest show cave complex in Western Europe.

Cardiff: Techniquest (0222) 460211. Open Tue–Sun, holidays daily. Hands-on science and technology centre.

Llanwrda: Dolaucothi Goldmines, Pumsaint, National Trust (05585) 359. Open daily Apr–Oct, Underground tours May–Sept. Originally exploited 2000 years ago by Romans – Miners Way walk – underground tours except for under 5 year olds – other guided walks on request.

Laugharne: Dylan Thomas Boat House (0994) 427420. Open Apr–Nov daily, winter Sun–Fri. Boathouse above Tâf estuary – Heritage Centre.

Further reading

General

Gower. The Journal of the Gower Society; published annually.
A Guide to Gower. The Gower Society; 5th edition 1982.
Balchin, W.G.V., ed. *Swansea and its Region*. University College of Swansea; 1971.
Jones, Roger. *Gower Fact and Fable*. Roger Jones.
Lucas, Robert. *Rhossili*. D Brown & Sons Ltd; 1989.
Phillips, Olive. *Gower*. Robert Hale Ltd; 1956.
Vaughan Thomas, Wynford. *Portrait of Gower*. Robert Hale Ltd; 1976.

Geology

Neville George, T. *British Regional Geology South Wales*. HMSO; 1970; 2nd impression 1975.
Trueman, A.E. *Geology and Scenery in England and Wales*. Penguin; 1949, revised 1971.

Natural History

Berney, Julia. *A Guide to Gower Seashore*. Culver House Press; 1985.
Gillham, Mary E. *The Natural History of Gower*. D Brown & Sons Ltd; 1977.
Grenfell, H.E. & Thomas, D.K. *A Guide to Gower Birds*. Gower Ornithological Society and Glamorgan Naturalists' Trust; 1982.
Goodman, Gordon T. *Plant Life in Gower*. The Gower Society.

Prehistory & History

Davis, Paul R. *Historic Gower*. Christopher Davis Ltd; 1986.
Grenfell, H.E. & Morris, B. *The Castles of Gower*. The Gower Society.
Grenfell, H.E. & Morris, B. *The Caves of Gower*. The Gower Society.
Rutter, J.G. *Prehistoric Gower*. Swansea; 1948.

Churches

Grenfell, H.E. & Toft, L.A. *Noteworthy Gower Churches*. The Gower Society.
Orrin, G.R. *The Gower Churches*. Swansea, The Rural Deanery of West Gower; 1979.

Llanddewi Church

79

THE FAMILY WALKS SERIES

Family Walks on Anglesey. Laurence Main. ISBN 0 907758 665.

Family Walks in Berkshire & North Hampshire. Kathy Sharp. ISBN 0 907758 371.

Family Walks around Bristol, Bath & the Mendips. Nigel Vile. ISBN 0 907758 193.

Family Walks around Cardiff & the Valleys. Gordon Hindess. ISBN 0 907758 541.

Family Walks in Cheshire. Chris Buckland. ISBN 0 907758 290.

Family Walks in Cornwall. John Caswell. ISBN 0 907758 55X.

Family Walks in the Cotswolds. Gordon Ottewell. ISBN 0 907758 150.

Family Walks on Exmoor & the Quantocks. John Caswell. ISBN 0 907758 460.

Family Walks in South Gloucestershire. Gordon Ottewell. ISBN 0 907758 339.

Family Walks in Gower. Amanda Green. ISBN 0 907758 630.

Family Walks in Hereford and Worcester. Gordon Ottewell. ISBN 0 907758 207.

Family Walks on the Isle of Wight. Laurence Main. ISBN 0 907758 568.

Family Walks in North West Kent. Clive Cutter. ISBN 0 907758 363.

Family Walks in the Lake District. Barry McKay. ISBN 0 907758 401.

Family Walks in Mendip, Avalon & Sedgemoor. Nigel Vile. ISBN 0 907758 41X.

Family Walks in the New Forest. Nigel Vile. ISBN 0 907758 606.

Family Walks in Oxfordshire. Laurence Main. ISBN 0 907758 38X.

Family Walks in the Dark Peak. Norman Taylor. ISBN 0 907758 169.

Family Walks in the White Peak. Norman Taylor. ISBN 0 907758 096.

Family Walks in South Derbyshire. Gordon Ottewell. ISBN 0 907758 614.

Family Walks in South Shropshire. Marian Newton. ISBN 0 907758 304.

Family Walks in Snowdonia. Laurence Main. ISBN 0 907758 320.

Family Walks in the Staffordshire Peaks and Potteries. Les Lumsdon. ISBN 0 907758 347.

Family Walks around Stratford & Banbury. Gordon Ottewell. ISBN 0 907758 495.

Family Walks in Suffolk. C J Francis. ISBN 0 907758 649.

Family Walks around Swansea. Raymond Humphreys. ISBN 0 907758 622.

Family Walks in the Teme Valley. Camilla Harrison. ISBN 0 907758 452.

Family Walks in Three Peaks & Malham. Howard Beck. ISBN 0 907758 428

Family Walks in Mid Wales. Laurence Main. ISBN 0 907758 274.

Family Walks in the North Wales Borderlands. Gordon Emery. ISBN 0 907758 509.

Family Walks in Warwickshire. Geoff Allen. ISBN 0 907758 533.

Family Walks in the Weald of Kent & Sussex. Clive Cutter. ISBN 0 907758 517.

Family Walks in Wiltshire. Nigel Vile. ISBN 0 907758 215.

Family Walks in the Wye Valley. Heather & Jon Hurley. ISBN 0 907758 266.

Family Walks in the North Yorkshire Dales. Howard Beck. ISBN 0 907758 525.

Family Walks in South Yorkshire. Norman Taylor. ISBN 0 907758 258.

Family Walks in West Yorkshire. Howard Beck. ISBN 0 907758 436.

The publishers welcome suggestions for further titles in this series; and will be pleased to consider manuscripts relating to Derbyshire from new or established authors.

Scarthin Books of Cromford, in the Peak District, are also leading second-hand and antiquarian booksellers, and are eager to purchase specialised material, both ancient and modern.

Contact Dr D. J. Mitchell, 0629-823272.

THE HIVE BEACH CAFÉ
FAMILY COOKBOOK

DEDICATED TO THE ATTRILL FAMILY

RECIPES BY MAISY ATTRILL, MELANIE ATTRILL, TIM ATTRILL, HANNAH CLIFFORD, LEAH EARLE, JAMIE COOMBES, BARRY GEORGE, TIM GIBB & GILES GREENING.

EDITED BY RUFUS PURDY & SARAH MABER

PHOTOGRAPHY BY COLIN CRABB

INTRODUCTION

Our first book, *The Hive Beach Café Cookbook*, was a runaway hit. It found a place in both the kitchens of our wonderful local customers and of the holidaymakers who wanted to recreate an unforgettable dining experience at home. People loved its delicious, easy-to-follow recipes and its authenticity – this was sustainable Dorset food, sourced locally, cooked simply. The food at The Hive isn't messed about with.

So why the need for a second book? Of all the feedback we had, one point resonated. The recipes in *The Hive Beach Café Cookbook* were for two. Yet The Hive is a much-loved, family-run, family friendly café. We pride ourselves on catering for everyone, from grandparents to mums and dads, to children and babies. Even dogs are welcomed – we have a range of biscuits for them. Noisy, loving, sprawling lunches and dinners are what memories are made of. And so *The Hive Beach Café Family Cookbook* was born – a treasure trove of delicious recipes to be cooked, savoured and revisited again and again by different generations.

Food has always been a big part of my own family life. I was nine when my parents first took a pub in Bridport. At 18 I started training as a chef and, 20 years ago, I took over The Hive – which at the time had seating for just 12. Over the years, working closely with the village of Burton Bradstock as well as the National Trust, we have expanded and built up fantastic relationships with both our customers and our local suppliers.

As The Hive has grown in popularity, we have grown the business. We opened The Watch House Café last year, selling pizzas and seafood on the beach at West Bay. Families love it – we even lay on Punch and Judy shows for the kids in the summer. We have a bakery that produces every conceivable cake under the sun and an electric van that delivers the produce to The Watch House and The Hive. We sell puddings to farm shops, do a range of fantastic sandwiches and have just started selling our famous seasonings. Our 50-year-old converted Airstream Trailer means we can now cater for large groups away from The Hive. We have rickshaws that run around West Bay and very soon we'll be selling our own artisan ice cream.

Great food for the whole family is at the heart of everything we do and we hope you and your family get a lot of pleasure from this book. Please do let us know what you think.

Steve Attrill, Burton Bradstock, December 2013

CONTENTS

BREAKFASTS

SALADS & SOUPS

SANDWICHES & LIGHT BITES

STYLISH SUPPERS

CONTENTS

SPECIAL OCCASIONS

PIZZAS

CROWD-PLEASERS

CAKES & PUDDINGS

HOW TO PREPARE FISH

ENSURING YOUR FISH IS FRESH

- Are the eyes clear? Avoid any fish that has cloudy, dull-looking eyes.
- Is the skin firm and shiny? If it's soft to the touch, then move on.
- Are the gills red and clear? Don't touch anything with cloudy slime around this area.
- Is it odourless? If the fish has a strong smell, then it's past its best.
- Does the fish feel wet and is its clear, slimy protective covering still evident? Avoid if not.

CHECKING YOUR FISH IS COOKED

- If you are cooking a whole fish – or an unfilleted portion – you can tell whether or not it's ready by inserting a small knife into the section nearest the bones, and checking the flesh has changed from a translucent colour to a more solid (usually white) one.

- If you're using fillets (ie, bone-free portions) of fish, there are two ways to check whether they're ready to eat. The first is to insert a small knife into the flesh at the centre of the fillet and look to see whether it has changed from a translucent colour to a more solid one. The second – which we recommend for thicker fillets – is to insert a knife into the centre, then withdraw it and place it flat on the back of your hand. If the knife is hot, the fillet will be cooked.

HOW·TO PREPARE FISH

FILLETING, SCALING & PIN-BONING

● Filleting refers to removing the main part of the skeleton, leaving you with a portion of fish that's relatively bone-free. Pin-boning refers to the more intricate job of removing any bones that are left after filleting.
● When filleting, make sure you use a sharp knife; and always direct the knife away from you as this will avert injury should it slip.
● Scaling refers to the messy task of scraping away the fish's scales with a knife. This is done from tail to head, working against the grain of the scales. We recommend using a palette knife when scaling, as – thanks to its blunt edges – it's unlikely to break the skin. At The Hive, we also use scallop shells, which work surprisingly well.

FILLETING A FLATFISH

● With a sharp filleting knife, cut along the sides of the fish's head down to the bone.
● Cut along the back of the fish, from head to tail, following the line of the fish's slightly raised backbone.
● Carefully cut the flesh away from each side of the backbone, keeping your knife flat and as close to the bones as possible. Fold the flesh back as you do so. This will produce two fillets.
● Turn the fish over and repeat the process on the other side.

FILLETING A ROUNDFISH

● Scale the fish with a knife or scallop shell. Carefully scrape from the tail towards the head to remove scales, but be careful not to break the skin. Repeat the process on the other side.
● With a sharp filleting knife, cut around the fish's head down to the bone.
● Cut back into the fish, following the spine-line, and carefully remove the fillet from the bone. Fold the flesh back as you work your way along the fish. This will produce one fillet.
● Remove any bones that are left and trim the fillet.
● Turn the fish over and repeat the process on the other side.

HOW TO PREPARE SEAFOOD & SHELLFISH

SQUID

● Take the squid's head in one hand and the body in the other, and gently pull. The head, along with the intestines, should come away easily. Cut the tentacles from the head.
● Squeeze the beak out from the middle of the tentacles, and discard it.
● Insert your hand into the body pouch and pull out the plasticky quill and any roe.
● Pull the two fins from either side of the body pouch, then pull off the translucent skin.
● Rinse the pouch thoroughly with cold water.

CRAB

● Bring a pan of salted water up to the boil.
● Kill your crab by first inserting a skewer between its eyes. Then turn it over and push a skewer into the small pointed flap towards the back of its shell. Give the skewer a sharp tap, so that you feel it hit the other side of the shell.
● Place the crab in the boiling water for 10 minutes, then turn off the heat and allow it to cool in the water.
● Once the crab has cooled, take it out from the pan, and remove and discard the grey, feathery gills (known as dead man's fingers) from the underside of the body.

HOW TO PREPARE SEAFOOD & SHELLFISH

LOBSTER

- Place your lobster into the freezer for 2 hours before you need it.
- When you're ready to start cooking, bring a pan of salted water up to the boil and add the lobster straight from the freezer. Boil it for 10 minutes then allow it to cool in the water.
- Cut the lobster in half lengthways with a sharp knife. Remove the dark intestinal tract that runs down the middle, then get rid of the green-coloured liver and any roe.
- Use a hammer or nutcrackers to break the hard shell of the claws and access the meat.

MUSSELS & CLAMS

- When buying mussels or clams, make sure that they are still alive. Discard any that are open and do not close when tapped, and get rid of ones with shells that are cracked or damaged.
- Rinse your mussels or clams in cold water to remove any dirt.
- Use a knife to scrape off any barnacles or persistent dirt from the shells.
- Pull out any beards – the fibrous strands that protrude from the shells – and rinse once more in cold running water. They are now ready to cook.

HOW TO
PREPARE SEAFOOD
& SHELLFISH

OYSTERS

● When buying oysters, make sure that they are still alive. They should feel heavy – live oysters carry a lot of water. Discard any that are open and do not close when tapped, and get rid of ones with shells that are cracked or damaged.

● Shucking – ie, opening – an oyster can be dangerous. At The Hive, we always place a tea towel over the hand in which we hold the oyster to prevent injury should the knife slip.

● Hold an oyster with the flatter side facing upwards, then take an oyster knife and push it into the hinge – the narrowest point – of the oyster. Be careful not to push too hard or the knife might slip.

● Twist the knife and lift off the top of the oyster shell. Remove this – taking care not to let any fragments fall into the bottom half – and free the oyster, which will be attached by a muscle to the shell.

● An oyster that is good to eat will smell clean and fresh when you open it. The liquid inside the shell should be clear rather than cloudy.

SCALLOPS

● When buying scallops, try to source hand-dived ones rather than the more common dredged variety. They are much cleaner, as well as being more environmentally friendly.

● Rinse your scallops in cold running water to get rid of any dirt.

● Gently ease open the scallop shell with a knife or other flat blade.

● Carefully slide the blade between the scallop and the top half of the shell, and cut through the piece of ligament that attaches the two.

● Repeat this process with the bottom half of the shell.

● Remove the unappetising black stomach sac, as well as any dirt and 'skirt', from the scallop, leaving just the white flesh and coral intact. It is now ready to cook.

HOW TO MAKE STOCKS, SAUCES & ACCOMPANIMENTS

FISH STOCK

INGREDIENTS

Butter

Olive oil

2 onions, sliced

1 stick celery, chopped

1 leek, sliced

1 fennel bulb, sliced

1kg fish bones (flatfish bones work best)

Glass white wine

2 bay leaves

6 black peppercorns

Sprig thyme

Small bunch parsley, chopped

● Melt a knob of butter and a drizzle of olive oil in a large saucepan, and sweat the onions until soft. Add the celery, leek and fennel, and cook for another couple of minutes.

● Add the fish bones and white wine, and cook until the liquid has reduced by half. Put in the bay leaves, peppercorns, thyme and parsley, and cover with water. Bring up to a gentle simmer and cook for 20 minutes, skimming regularly.

● Strain through a muslin-lined sieve. The fish stock is now ready to use.

MAYONNAISE

INGREDIENTS

2 egg yolks

2 tsp white wine vinegar

1 tsp Dijon mustard

300ml rapeseed oil

● Place the egg yolks, white wine vinegar and Dijon mustard into a food processor, along with sea salt and freshly ground black pepper, and blend until pale and creamy.

● Pour in the rapeseed oil in a steady stream, blending continually, until the mayonnaise reaches a thick consistency.

HOW TO MAKE STOCKS, SAUCES & ACCOMPANIMENTS

TARTARE SAUCE

INGREDIENTS

100ml mayonnaise (see opposite)
Small handful pickled gherkins, chopped
Small handful pickled capers, chopped

Bunch flat-leaf parsley, chopped
½ red onion, finely diced
1 lemon, juiced

● Place the mayonnaise in a mixing bowl, then add the gherkins, capers, parsley, red onion and lemon juice. Mix well.
● Season with sea salt and freshly ground black pepper, then set aside in the fridge.

HOLLANDAISE SAUCE

INGREDIENTS

½ shallot, finely diced
100ml white wine
75ml white wine vinegar

1 bay leaf
250g butter
2 egg yolks

● Place the shallot, white wine, white wine vinegar, bay leaf and some freshly ground black pepper into a sauté pan, and bring to the boil.
● Simmer until the liquid has reduced by three-quarters, then strain it through a sieve and set aside in a warm place.
● Melt the butter in a small pan and allow it to boil for around 1 minute, until the fats separate. Let it cool for 1 minute or so, until the butter fat sinks to the bottom, then set aside.
● Pour the egg yolks into a mixing bowl, then add the reduced, sieved wine liquid. Blend together with a hand blender, then slowly pour in the clear, clarified butter (not the milky butter fat) while blending continually. Don't pour too fast, otherwise the sauce will split.
● Stop adding the clarified butter when the sauce reaches a thick consistency.

HOW TO MAKE PIZZA DOUGH & TOMATO SAUCE

PIZZA DOUGH

INGREDIENTS

4 tbsp olive oil

1 tbsp caster sugar

2 7g packets yeast

650ml lukewarm water

1kg Tipo 00 flour or strong white-bread flour

● Add the olive oil, sugar and yeast to the water and mix. Set aside for a few minutes.

● Sieve the flour and a pinch of sea salt onto a clean work surface and make a well in the centre. Pour the water-and-yeast mixture into the well and slowly incorporate the flour. Knead until you have a smooth-looking, elastic-feeling dough.

● Put the dough in a large bowl and cover it with a slightly damp tea towel. Set aside in a warm place for 45 minutes to 1 hour until it has doubled in size.

● Return the dough to a clean work surface and knead again. Split into the number of portions you require (at The Watch House, we use around 180g for each pizza base). Wrap any dough you're not using immediately in clingfilm and set aside in the fridge.

TOMATO & BASIL SAUCE

INGREDIENTS

400g chopped tomatoes

80g tomato purée

40ml olive oil

½ tsp dried oregano

10–15 fresh basil leaves

2 cloves garlic, crushed

● Put the tomatoes, tomato purée, olive oil, oregano and basil into a bowl with 1 heaped tsp sea salt and a twist of black pepper and blitz with a hand-held blender. Stop as soon as you've combined the oil.

● Mix in the garlic and set aside in the fridge. The longer you leave the sauce, the more the flavour of the garlic will infuse it. This recipe makes enough sauce for 6–8 pizzas.

BREAKFASTS

TALL PANCAKE STACK WITH CRISPY BACON

SERVES 4

This all-American breakfast tastes just as good on this side of the Atlantic and, though preparing all those pancakes can be a little time-consuming, the cooking process is one children will enjoy. Tossing pancakes, after all, is one of the most theatrical ways of putting a meal together. As always, the quality of the ingredients is key to this dish. Go for thick-cut bacon from your butcher, which won't shrink under the grill, and make sure you use free-range eggs.

INGREDIENTS

12 rashers bacon
270g plain flour
2 tsp baking powder
2 tbsp caster sugar

2 large eggs
260ml milk
4 tbsp clarified butter
Maple syrup

- Preheat a frying pan over a low heat. Warm up a hot grill.
- Place the bacon rashers on a baking tray and grill until crispy. Set aside in a warm place.
- Sift the flour and baking powder into a bowl, then add the sugar, eggs, milk and 4 tbsp clarified butter. Season with a little salt and whisk the mixture together into a thick batter.
- Spoon a ladleful of the batter into the frying pan and rotate so that it covers the base. Cook for a couple of minutes until the pancake is golden on the bottom, then toss it and cook the other side for a couple of minutes more. Set the pancake aside in a warm place and repeat until you have a stack of 12 pancakes or more.
- Arrange the crispy bacon between the layers of the pancake stack and finish with a generous drizzle of maple syrup. Serve immediately and watch everyone get stuck in.

BUBBLE & SQUEAK

SERVES 4

A classic British breakfast (though we've also been known to serve it for dinner), bubble and squeak is the ultimate thrifty meal. Leftover mashed potato, carrots, cabbage and spring greens? Simply chuck 'em in a warm, buttered pan, add a handful of cheese and voilá; perfect hangover fodder for you and comfort food for the kids. At The Hive, we like to make use of the sea kale and sea beet that grows all around us on the Dorset coast and we've found these foraged ingredients add a beautiful, fresh taste to the traditional combination. The beauty of this dish, though, is that you can add whatever you like.

INGREDIENTS

4 large potatoes, peeled and chopped
4 portions vine-on cherry tomatoes
Olive oil
1 bunch sea kale
Butter

Handful wild sea beet (or spinach)
Handful cheddar, grated
Handful parsley, chopped
Bunch wild watercress

- Preheat a hot grill and warm up a frying pan.
- Boil the potatoes until soft, then drain and mash. Set aside in a warm place.
- Brush the cherry tomatoes with a little olive oil and season with sea salt and freshly ground black pepper, then place under the grill. Cook until soft then set aside in a warm place.
- Remove the stems from the sea kale and slice the leaves thinly. Melt a knob of butter in the frying pan, then add the sea kale and cook gently for 3–4 minutes.
- Once the sea kale is ready, add the mashed potato and sea beet to the pan and continue cooking. Throw in the cheddar after a couple of minutes and fry until the mash is a golden-brown colour all over. Check the mixture is piping-hot throughout.
- Sprinkle parsley over the top and serve immediately with the wild watercress and the vine-on cherry tomatoes.

SMOKED MACKEREL KEDGEREE

SERVES 4

Kedgeree may have its origins in the days of the Raj, but this moreish combination of smoked fish, rice and spices goes down just as well on a chilly afternoon in Burton Bradstock as it does on a sultry morning in Bombay. At The Hive, we also make the dish with the more traditional smoked haddock – though since the opening of The Chesil Smokery in Bridport, we've erred towards creating it with the wonderfully oily, oak and apple-smoked mackerel fillets it produces. We've found that kids love this mild dish just as much as adults, but you can always reduce the amount of curry powder in this recipe if you're worried about the heat.

INGREDIENTS

2 eggs
Pinch cumin seeds
Pinch mustard seeds
1 onion, chopped
1 tbsp sunflower oil
1½ tbsp curry powder

200g long-grain rice
2 smoked mackerel fillets, skin removed
and flaked
Handful coriander, chopped
Dollop crème fraîche
1 lemon, cut into wedges

● Bring a pan of water to the boil and put the eggs in gently to prevent them cracking. Boil for 7 minutes, then place straight into cold water to prevent the yolks from going grey. Peel the eggs once they've cooled and set aside in the fridge.
● Toast the cumin and mustard seeds in a dry frying pan, then crush in a pestle and mortar.
● In a pan, sweat the onion in the sunflower oil and cook until soft. Add the crushed spices and curry powder, and cook for another minute.
● Add the rice to the pan, then cover with water (2cm above the level of the mixture). Bring to the boil and simmer for 10–12 minutes, until the rice is soft.
● Once you're happy with consistency of the rice, add in the smoked mackerel flakes, coriander and crème fraîche. Heat until the dish is warm throughout, then serve garnished with the chopped boiled eggs and a squeeze of lemon.

EGGY BREAD WITH STREAKY BACON

SERVES 4

So easy to prepare, yet packing a serious punch in terms of flavour, this version of the nursery-food classic has long been a staple of our breakfast menu at The Hive. We use freshly baked bread from our own micro-bakery at West Bay, fresh Dorset farm eggs and streaky bacon from local pork suppliers to ensure a superior taste. And, if you don't mind your kitchen getting a little messy, this is a wonderful dish to prepare with children. Just make sure you've got some kitchen roll to hand to mop up the inevitable egg spillages.

INGREDIENTS

3 large eggs
4–8 thick slices bread

12 slices streaky bacon
Olive oil

- Preheat a hot grill and warm up a frying pan.
- Crack the eggs into a large bowl and whisk, then dip each slice of bread into the mixture to coat them thoroughly.
- Lay the streaky bacon slices out on a tray and grill until crisp. Set aside in a warm place.
- Drizzle a little olive oil into the frying pan, then add the egg-coated slices of bread (you may need to do this in two batches). Fry until the side in contact with the bottom of the pan is golden-brown, then turn and fry the other side.
- Arrange on 4 plates and top each with 3 slices of crisp bacon. Serve immediately.

SCRAMBLED RHEA'S EGG SERVED IN THE SHELL

SERVES 4

A rhea is a large, flightless bird – a little like an ostrich – which can be found on the plains of South America. So why are we serving its eggs (equivalent in size to 10 hens' eggs) here on the south coast of England? Well, we were delighted to discover that these huge birds are being bred locally and – after visiting the farm – we couldn't resist experimenting with the produce. The result is one of the more out-there dishes on our breakfast menu; but it's been met with favourable responses whenever we've served it. If you can't get down to Dorset to pick some up, rheas' eggs are available at certain times of the year online from www.clarencecourt.co.uk.

INGREDIENTS

1 rhea's egg
Double cream

4–8 slices bread
Butter

- Preheat a hot grill and warm up a frying pan over a low heat.
- Take the rhea's egg and, with a knife, gently tap around the top in a line. The shell should crack easily.
- Pour the egg into a large bowl. Gently clean the inside of the shell and stand it in a small bowl. Set aside.
- Whisk the egg together with a dash of double cream. Season to taste.
- Toast the bread under the grill. While this is cooking, add a knob of butter to the frying pan and pour in the egg mixture. Cook for a few minutes, stirring occasionally, until you've achieved your ideal consistency.
- Remove the bread from the grill and cut into soldiers. Transfer the scrambled egg from the pan into the cleaned eggshell and serve immediately.

Photograph: Georgia Glynn-Smith

SKEWERED SCALLOPS WRAPPED IN PARMA HAM

MAKES 4 SKEWERS

Impressive, inventive and, most importantly, fun, these skewers make a family breakfast feel just a little bit special. Scallops tend to be a favourite with kids thanks to their delicate flavour and sheer attractiveness; wrap them in ham and savour the tasty blend of surf and turf. Throw in the sweet sharpness of roast tomatoes and the gooey comfort of a perfectly poached egg to make this an unforgettable meal. Or add some good toasted sourdough bread and lightly dressed watercress to turn this into a stylish dinner-party treat for grown-ups.

INGREDIENTS

White wine vinegar
4 portions vine-on cherry tomatoes
Olive oil

4 eggs
12 scallops
12 slices Parma ham

● Preheat your oven to 180°C/350°F. Bring a pan of water to the boil and add a splash of white wine vinegar. Warm up a large frying pan.
● Place the cherry tomatoes onto a baking tray and drizzle with olive oil, then season with sea salt and freshly ground black pepper. Bake in the oven till soft, then set aside in a warm place.
● Carefully crack the eggs into the pan of boiling water and poach for 2–3 minutes.
● Wrap each scallop in a slice of Parma ham, and arrange 3 onto each skewer. Coat in olive oil and pan-fry till golden-brown on all sides.
● Place each skewer onto a plate, arrange the baked cherry tomatoes alongside and finish with a poached egg. Serve immediately.

SMOKED HADDOCK FRITATTA

SERVES 4

Incredibly popular in the café, particularly on a misty Dorset morning, this family breakfast favourite has it all – smoked fish, sharp and creamy cheddar cheese and fresh herbs – and, thanks to its one-pan preparation method, it even saves on the washing up. We use smoked haddock from Bridport's The Chesil Smokery and Ashley Chase cheddar (both of which we heartily recommend), but feel free to source your own local ingredients.

INGREDIENTS

8 large eggs
Handful chives, chopped
50ml double cream
Handful spinach, washed
Butter

Vegetable oil
350g smoked haddock
50g cheddar, grated
Handful wild rocket

- Preheat a hot grill and warm up a large frying pan.
- Whisk the eggs, chives and double cream together with a pinch of sea salt and freshly ground black pepper. Stir in the spinach.
- Melt a knob of butter in the frying pan with a drizzle of vegetable oil, and gently fry the smoked haddock until it has cooked through. Be careful not to overcook otherwise the fish will start to break apart.
- Add the spinach and egg mixture to the pan and cook for 3–5 minutes, until the frittata base has cooked and begins to crisp.
- Scatter the cheddar over the top and place the pan under the grill until the cheese has melted and the top of the frittata has turned a golden-brown colour.
- Top with wild rocket and serve immediately.

PAN-FRIED SCALLOPS WITH PANCETTA & BLACK PUDDING

SERVES 4

The fabulous combination of delicate, straight-out-of-the-sea Lyme Bay scallops and dense, earthy black pudding is one we cottoned on to early at The Hive. And, though the dish can now be found in virtually every restaurant and café within reach of a decent fishmonger, we keep it on the breakfast menu for the simple reason that it's absolutely delicious – especially when topped with crisp, salty pancetta. It's worth spending a bit more to get a really good black pudding from your local butcher – the supermarket-bought ones just aren't the same.

INGREDIENTS

White wine vinegar
4 slices pancetta
1 black pudding
Olive oil

4 eggs
12 scallops
Handful wild rocket

● Preheat a hot grill and warm up a heavy-bottomed frying pan. Bring a pan of water to the boil and add a splash of white wine vinegar.

● Lay the pancetta slices out on a tray and grill until crisp. Set aside in a warm place.

● Cut the black pudding into 4 chunky slices and brush each lightly with olive oil. Grill for 2–3 minutes on each side, until they're cooked through. Set aside in a warm place.

● Carefully crack the eggs into the pan of boiling water and poach for 2–3 minutes.

● Season the scallops with sea salt and olive oil, and place them into the hot frying pan. Turn each scallop after 45–60 seconds (depending on their size). Make sure the scallops are golden-brown where they've been in contact with pan and have an even colour on both sides.

● To serve, arrange 3 scallops on a plate, add a slice of black pudding, a poached egg and wild rocket, and finish with the crisp pancetta.

BLUEBERRY PANCAKES WITH FRESH FRUIT & VANILLA MASCARPONE

SERVES 4

These delicious, easy-to-make, fruit-stacked pancakes are regularly ordered and devoured by families at The Hive. While any seasonal, soft fruit will work, this particular blend of berries, kiwi and passion fruit brings an unusual depth of flavour to breakfast times. To serve, place the pancakes in a stack on the bottom of a plate, add fruit and finish with vanilla mascarpone and a drizzle of balsamic glaze. It's impressive, easy and indulgent.

INGREDIENTS

½ punnet strawberries

1 punnet raspberries

2 kiwi fruit, skin removed

4 passion fruit, skin removed

½ vanilla pod

4 tbsp mascarpone

270g plain flour

2 tsp baking powder

2 tbsp caster sugar

2 large eggs

260ml milk

4 tbsp clarified butter

1 punnet blueberries

Balsamic vinegar

● Preheat a frying pan over a low heat.

● Prepare the fresh fruit by topping and halving the strawberries and raspberries, and chopping the kiwi and passion fruit into small pieces. Mix together in a large bowl.

● Mix the vanilla pod and the mascarpone together.

● Sift the flour and baking powder into a bowl, then add the sugar, eggs, milk and clarified butter. Season with a little salt and whisk together into a thick batter. Add the blueberries.

● Spoon a ladleful of the batter into the frying pan and rotate so that it covers the base. Cook for a couple of minutes until the pancake is golden on the bottom, then toss it and cook the other side for a couple of minutes more.

● Stack the pancakes on a large plate, and top with the fresh fruit and vanilla mascarpone. For a final touch, pour a little balsamic vinegar into the frying pan in which you've cooked the pancakes and turn up the heat. Let it bubble for a couple of minutes, then drizzle the glaze over the pancake stack. Serve immediately.

MESSY BACON CIABATTA

MAKES 4 SANDWICHES

If you're undecided about what to have for breakfast, then this dish is ideal – it contains pretty much everything you've ever wanted: bacon, eggs, cheese and rocket. At The Hive, we like to use deliciously tangy Ashley Chase cheddar in our cheese sauce, as it gives the sandwich an extra boost of taste. But any good farmhouse cheddar will suffice. Serve these sandwiches up with a pot of tea or a cafetière of strong coffee, and don't forget to put plenty of napkins out. We don't call this the messy bacon ciabatta for nothing.

INGREDIENTS

25g butter
25g plain flour
100ml milk
150g cheddar, grated
1 tsp wholegrain mustard
Splash Worcester sauce

White wine vinegar
4 ciabattas, cut in half
12 rashers bacon
4 eggs
Handful wild rocket

● First make the cheese sauce. Melt the butter in a saucepan, then add the flour and cook for 20 seconds. Pour in the milk and bring the mixture up to a gentle simmer. Continue simmering for 2 minutes, then add the cheddar, mustard and Worcester sauce. Once all the cheese has melted into the sauce, remove it from the heat and set aside. You can make this sauce up to a day in advance.
● Bring a pan of water up to the boil and add a splash of white wine vinegar. Preheat a grill.
● Toast the ciabattas under the grill then set aside in a warm place. Place the bacon rashers on a baking tray and grill until cooked through.
● Carefully crack the eggs into the pan of boiling water and poach for 2–3 minutes.
● Spread the cheese sauce onto the ciabattas and grill until golden-brown.
● Arrange 3 rashers of bacon, a poached egg and wild rocket onto the bottom half of each ciabatta and serve immediately.

SALADS &
SOUPS

MUSSEL & SAFFRON SOUP

SERVES 4

This simple, fragrant soup can be served as an easy (but impressive) lunch or supper for family and friends. Mussels are often overlooked by those in charge of planning the family meals, which is a shame. They are cheap, quick to cook and their delicate flavour can elevate a standard supper into something special; adding a few saffron strands infuses this soup with a gorgeous golden colour. Best of all, you can have this ready to eat in about 10 minutes. Don't forget to top with a generous scattering of parsley and serve with fresh, crusty bread.

INGREDIENTS

1kg mussels
1 onion, roughly chopped
1 clove garlic, roughly chopped
Butter

2 pinches saffron strands
Glass white wine
240ml single cream
Handful parsley, chopped

● Wash the mussels in cold water and discard any that do not close when tapped.
● Sweat the onion and garlic along with a knob of butter in a heavy-based saucepan until soft. Add the mussels and saffron strands, cook for around a minute more, then add the white wine and a glass of water. Steam until the mussels have opened. Discard any that remain closed.
● Drain the mussels – ensuring you retain the cooking liquid.
● Bring the cooking liquid up to the boil, add the single cream and reduce it until it has thickened slightly.
● Add the mussels back into the soup, bring back to the boil then serve immediately, sprinkled with chopped parsley.

GREEK SALAD WITH CHARGRILLED GILTHEAD BREAM

SERVES 4

The delicate flavour and firm texture of gilthead bream – a cheap and sustainable alternative to the red mullet or swordfish you would usually associate with Greek cuisine – is an ideal match to the sharpness of the feta cheese and olives in this classic Mediterranean salad. Great for a quick – and impressive – family lunch, this dish is best eaten outdoors; ideally beneath a warm sun and with the sound of the sea in the background. Serve it with a chilled bottle of crisp white wine and plenty of crusty bread.

INGREDIENTS

Olive oil

1 fillet gilthead bream, scaled and pin-boned

1 block feta, cubed

3 beef tomatoes, sliced

1 red onion, finely chopped

Oregano

2 lemons, cut into wedges

Your favourite salad dressing

4–6 handfuls mixed salad leaves

50g black olives, pitted

50g green olives, pitted

● Preheat a chargrill or griddle pan over a high heat until it's smoking-hot. Preheat your oven to 180°C/350°F. Oil and season the gilthead bream fillet.

● Place the gilthead bream onto the chargrill. Wait until the side in contact with the chargrill turns a golden-brown colour, then remove the fillet and place it on an oiled baking tray. Bake in the oven for 4–5 minutes.

● While the fish is cooking, prepare the Greek salad. Put the feta in a mixing bowl with the tomatoes, red onion, a sprinkle of oregano, a squeeze of lemon and a splash of salad dressing. Add the salad leaves and black and green olives, and mix thoroughly. Place in a large serving bowl.

● Allow the gilthead bream to rest for a few minutes, then place it on top of the salad. Serve with lemon wedges on the side.

LEEK & POTATO SOUP WITH SMOKED MACKEREL

SERVES 4

You can't go wrong with this flavoursome soup. Add the savoury hit of smoked mackerel to the classic leek-and-potato combo for a deeply satisfying, tasty lunch or supper; even young kids will wolf it down. At The Hive, we use hot-smoked mackerel from Bridport's The Chesil Smokery to guarantee a rich, warming flavour in this soup; flake it in towards the end of the cooking time and serve up the steaming dishes with warm granary bread on the side.

INGREDIENTS

1 onion, sliced
2 leeks, sliced
Butter
250g potatoes, peeled and chopped

1.15l vegetable stock
150ml single cream
2 smoked mackerel, skinned and flaked
Handful chives, chopped

● Sweat the onion and leeks with a knob of butter in a heavy-based saucepan until soft.

● Add the potatoes and cook for around a minute, then pour in the stock and bring to the boil. Gently simmer until the potatoes are cooked. They are ready when you insert a thin knife into them and they slip off easily. Set a couple of potatoes aside to use as a garnish.

● Pour in the cream and bring back to the boil. Season to taste, then blitz with a hand-held blender or in a food processor.

● Return the soup to the pan (if, indeed, you took it out in the first place), then add the flakes of smoked mackerel and the chives. Gently reheat until the mackerel is warm.

● Pour the soup into 4 bowls and finish each with a drizzle of cream and the reserved potatoes. Serve with hunks of crusty bread.

CRAB, ASPARAGUS & POMEGRANATE SALAD

SERVES 4

We serve a lot of crab at The Hive and The Watch House. Being located so close to the sea means they're super-fresh when they arrive (usually brought in by local fisherman Steve Elsworth) into our kitchen. Over the years, we've dished crabs up in many ways, but this salad is one of our favourite creations, especially when asparagus is in season in the southwest. The chargrill gives the spears a deliciously smoky flavour that works incredibly well with the crab meat.

INGREDIENTS

Olive oil

2 bunches asparagus, woody ends removed

1 crab, to yield 100g white meat and 100g brown meat

2 lemons, cut into wedges

2 pomegranates

4–6 handfuls mixed salad leaves

Your favourite salad dressing

● Preheat a chargrill or griddle pan over a high heat until it's smoking-hot. Preheat your oven to 180°C/350°F. Oil and season the asparagus spears.

● Place the asparagus onto the chargrill. As soon as the spears have coloured on one side, turn them over. Keep an eye on them as they cook very quickly. Set aside.

● Prepare the crab according to the instructions on page 12 or, alternatively, ask your fishmonger to do it for you. Drop the white crab meat onto a metal tray to see if it still contains any shell.

● Mix the crab meat together, add a squeeze of lemon and season with sea salt. Set aside in the fridge.

● Cut the pomegranates in half. Hold each half in your hand, seed-side down, and hit the top with the back of a wooden spoon to release the seeds. Set aside.

● Put the asparagus into the oven to warm through.

● Place the pomegranate seeds into a large bowl, then add the salad leaves and a generous drizzle of salad dressing. Mix well.

● Divide the salad between 4 bowls and top with a heaped tbsp of the mixed crab meat. Arrange the asparagus spears around the edge and serve immediately with lemon wedges.

CAULIFLOWER SOUP WITH CURRIED SCALLOPS

SERVES 4

Cauliflower and curried scallops may not seem an obvious pairing but, believe us, the spiciness of the curry powder, turmeric, coriander and cumin seeds combines wonderfully with the sweetness of the cauliflower and scallops. This is a simple, luxurious soup; the thick, velvety texture holds the scallops in place when you serve. Be careful not to overdo the scallops – fry briefly on each side, and aim for a golden-brown colour. And buy local scallops if you can; we source ours from Lyme Bay.

INGREDIENTS

Olive oil
1 onion, finely chopped
1 large cauliflower, chopped
1 tsp cumin seeds
1 tsp coriander seeds

1 tsp turmeric
1l stock (chicken or vegetable)
Double cream
16 scallops
2 tsp curry powder

● Heat a couple of tablespoons of olive oil in a large saucepan and cook the onion and cauliflower until soft. Add the cumin and coriander seeds, and the turmeric.

● Pour in the stock and a splash of double cream, and bring to the boil. Simmer for 10 minutes.

● Remove the soup from the heat and blitz with a hand-held blender or in a food processor. Season to taste and set aside in a warm place.

● Preheat a large frying pan. Place the scallops on a plate and season with the curry powder and sea salt.

● Drizzle a little olive oil into the frying pan then add the scallops; arrange them in a clockwise direction, remembering your starting point. After around 90 seconds, turn the scallops over in the same order.

● Reduce the heat to low and cook the scallops for another 90 seconds. Then remove in the same order as you put them into the pan to ensure they're evenly cooked. They should be golden-brown on both sides.

● Pour the soup into 4 bowls and add 4 scallops to each. Serve immediately.

PEAR, PEACH, MOZZARELLA & PARMESAN SALAD

SERVES 4

A lovely, fresh-tasting salad that's perfect for a family lunch – ideally outdoors with the sun warming the backs of everyone's necks. As always, good-quality ingredients are essential: the more local the pears are to you, the better; and we think it's well worth splashing out a little bit more to use buffalo mozzarella and proper Italian Parmesan. Be sparing with the honey in the salad dressing – you don't want to make it too sweet.

INGREDIENTS

25ml white wine vinegar
1 tbsp wholegrain mustard
1 tbsp Dijon mustard
75ml olive oil
1 tbsp honey

4–6 handfuls mixed salad leaves
6 peaches, destoned and cut into segments
6 pears, cut into long strips
6 balls mozzarella, cut into chunks
50g Parmesan, shaved

● To make the salad dressing, put the white wine vinegar, and wholegrain and Dijon mustards into a bowl, and mix with a hand-held blender. Pour in the olive oil in a steady stream, blending continually, until the dressing reaches a thick consistency. Add the honey.
● Place the salad leaves into a large bowl and pour in a little of the dressing. Mix to ensure all the leaves are covered, then add the peaches, pears and mozzarella.
● Divide the salad into 4 bowls and arrange Parmesan shavings on top of each. Drizzle with a little more dressing and serve.

HADDOCK & WHITE BEAN SOUP

SERVES 4

Soft and buttery white beans and salty haddock make for a fabulous combination – and this gorgeous, garlicky soup makes just as wonderful a dinner-party starter as it does a family teatime staple. You can either soak your beans overnight or – to save time – simply use canned white beans; either haricot or cannellini will work beautifully. Blend with roasted garlic, thyme and milk for a rich texture and crown each bowl of soup with a chunk of grilled haddock fillet. Delicious.

INGREDIENTS

2 bulbs garlic
Olive oil
1 onion, finely chopped
1 sprig thyme

800g white beans
150ml chicken stock
500ml milk
2 haddock fillets, skinned and pin-boned

● Preheat your oven to 180°C/350°F. Peel off the outer layers of the garlic bulbs (leaving the skin on each clove), then slice off the top of each bulb. Place onto an oiled roasting tray and roast in the oven for 25–30 minutes until the garlic is golden-brown and soft.

● Once cooled slightly, squeeze out the garlic cloves from their skin and set aside.

● Drizzle a little olive oil into a large saucepan and sweat the garlic, onion and thyme for a couple of minutes.

● Strain and rinse the beans, then add to the pan along with the chicken stock and milk. Bring to the boil then simmer for 10 minutes.

● Preheat a hot grill. Blitz the soup with a hand-held blender or in a food processor then season to taste. Set aside in a warm place.

● Cut each of your haddock fillets in two lengthways. Place onto an oiled and seasoned roasting tray and grill until cooked through.

● Divide the soup between 4 bowls and top each with a chunk of the grilled haddock. Serve immediately.

LOBSTER CAESAR SALAD

SERVES 4

A delicious and indulgent twist on the classic chicken Caesar salad, our seafood version – made at the café with lobsters plucked from the waters just off Hive Beach – is as popular with kids as it is with adults. We've seen children as young as four tuck into this dish with relish. And why not? The lobster meat is sweet and juicy, and the creamy dressing has that distinctive Parmesan tang. At The Hive, we like to serve this dish topped with strips of crispy pancetta and sprinkled with croutons made from bread, olive oil and herbs. But this simple version more than holds its own.

INGREDIENTS

Mayonnaise (see page 15)
Dijon mustard
White pepper
White wine vinegar
25g Parmesan, grated

2 cooked lobsters, cooled
1 head romaine lettuce, roughly chopped
Handful cherry tomatoes
Handful flat-leaf parsley, chopped

● Prepare your mayonnaise according to the instructions on page 15. Season to taste with the mustard, sea salt and white pepper.

● Add 5 tbsp white wine vinegar and mix until the mayonnaise has thinned and become the consistency of a dressing. Add the Parmesan. Set aside.

● Remove the tails and claws from the lobsters. Crack the claws and cut the tails open with scissors. Extract the remaining meat from the lobsters and, along with the tail and claw meat, chop into smaller pieces and place in a large bowl.

● Add the lettuce, cherry tomatoes and flat-leaf parsley, then pour in the Caesar dressing in stages and mix.

● Once you're happy with the taste, divide the salad between 4 bowls and serve immediately.

PEA & HAM SOUP WITH MINT CRÈME FRAÎCHE

SERVES 4

Made with homecooked ham hock, this nourishing soup is hearty enough for a one-pot family lunch or supper. The hock needs to be cooked for a good length of time to make sure it's falling off the bone – but the good news is that, once it's ready, you can whiz this soup together in minutes. Young children will love dunking in chunks of crusty bread and the robust, farmhouse flavour will keep everyone satisfied.

INGREDIENTS

1 ham hock	Olive oil
1 clove	Butter
2 black peppercorns	400g frozen peas
1 bay leaf	2 sprigs mint
1 onion, sliced	250g crème fraîche

● Place the ham hock in a large saucepan and cover with water. Add the clove, peppercorns and bay leaf, and bring to the boil. Simmer for 4–6 hours, topping up the water occasionally, until the ham is soft and falling off the bone.

● Remove the ham hock and set aside to cool. Strain the cooking liquid and retain.

● Sweat the onion in a large saucepan along with a drizzle of olive oil and a knob of butter until soft.

● Add the cooking liquid and bring to the boil. Then add the frozen peas, bring back to the boil and simmer for a couple of minutes until the peas have cooked.

● Remove from the heat and blitz with a hand-held blender or in a food processor.

● Trim any fat from the ham hock and pull the meat from the bone. Shred with a fork.

● Add the meat to the soup and warm it through.

● While the soup is heating, remove the leaves from the sprigs of mint and mix them into the crème fraîche.

● As soon as it's ready, pour the soup into 4 bowls and finish each with a spoonful of mint crème fraîche. Serve immediately.

SCALLOP & CHORIZO SALAD

SERVES 4

The piquant spiciness of chorizo and the delicate flavour of scallops has proved a wonderful combination time and again; and this teaming of tastes has established itself, over the past few years, as the British equivalent of the US surf and turf. This delicious salad works just as well for lunch as it does for an evening meal, and it's incredibly easy to prepare so long as you prepare all the ingredients and have them to hand. The cooking of the scallops and chorizo is – quite literally – a flash in the pan, and you don't want to be worrying about chopping while they're sizzling away.

INGREDIENTS

24–32 scallops, depending on size
Olive oil
1 chorizo, thinly sliced

1 head Romaine lettuce, chopped
Handful parsley, chopped
2 lemons, cut into wedges

● Preheat two heavy-bottomed frying pans. Season the scallops with sea salt and olive oil.
● Put the chorizo slices into one hot frying pan and cook until brown and crispy. Keep them moving to ensure they don't burn.
● Place the scallops into the other hot frying pan. Arrange them in a clockwise direction, remembering your starting point. After around 90 seconds, turn the scallops over in the same order. Add the chorizo to the pan.
● Reduce the heat to low and cook the scallops and chorizo for another 90 seconds. Then remove the scallops in the same order as you put them into the pan to ensure they're evenly cooked. They should be golden-brown on both sides.
● Put the lettuce and parsley in a large bowl then add the scallops. Squeeze in the juice of 1 lemon wedge. Add the lettuce and chorizo slices, and mix.
● Divide the salad between 4 bowls, ensuring that each contains 6–8 scallops, depending on size. Serve with lemon wedges on the side.

THAI KING PRAWN SOUP

SERVES 4

The delicate yet fiery taste of Thai soup goes down just as well in Burton Bradstock as it does in Bangkok and, when teamed with the fresh, meaty taste of king prawns, it is particularly wonderful – especially on a misty spring or autumn afternoon down on Hive Beach. We've found that kids love this soup just as much as adults, but your can always put in fewer chillies if you feel the fire-factor is too high for your family. Don't skimp on the prawns though. We've never heard of anyone asking for less of those.

INGREDIENTS

1 onion, finely chopped
Olive oil
800ml coconut milk
500ml chicken stock
2 sticks lemongrass, finely chopped
50g galangal, finely chopped
8 kaffir lime leaves, finely chopped

4 red chillies, finely chopped
500g large raw king prawns, peeled
Handful mange tout, finely chopped
Thai Nam Pla fish sauce
3 limes, juiced
3 basil leaves, chopped
Small handful coriander, chopped

● Sweat the onion in a large saucepan along with a drizzle of olive oil until soft. Then add the coconut milk and chicken stock, and bring to the boil. Turn down the heat to a simmer.
● Add the lemongrass, galangal, kaffir lime leaves, red chillies and king prawns, and simmer for a couple of minutes until the prawns are cooked.
● Put in the mange tout, then add a splash of Thai Nam Pla fish sauce and the lime juice. You can, at this stage, choose to blitz the mixture with a hand-held blender or in a food processor if you prefer a smooth soup. You will, though, need to return it to the pan to heat through before serving.
● Check the soup for seasoning then pour into 4 bowls. Sprinkle each with basil and coriander, and serve immediately.

SANDWICHES
& LIGHT BITES

LOBSTER CIABATTA WITH TARRAGON MAYONNAISE

MAKES 4 SANDWICHES

There are few sandwiches more indulgent than this one, filled to bursting with fresh lobster and creamy tarragon mayonnaise. Lobster may be a lot pricier than peanut butter, but the superior taste of this king of crustaceans is more than worth the extra expense. Kids, particularly, love the big-hitting flavours in these decadent lunchtime treats, and we suggest you serve it just as we do at The Hive – with the ciabattas still warm from the grill. You won't hear a word out of the family until the last mouthful has been swallowed.

INGREDIENTS

Mayonnaise (see page 15)
2 lobsters
2 sprigs tarragon, chopped
1 lemon, cut into wedges

4 ciabattas, cut in half lengthways
1 iceberg lettuce, chopped
Handful watercress

- Prepare your mayonnaise according to the instructions on page 15. Set aside.
- Next, prepare your lobsters according to the instructions on page 13. Preheat a grill.
- While the lobsters are cooling, combine the mayonnaise with the tarragon then add a good squeeze of lemon. Season to taste.
- Cut the lobsters in half lengthways and remove the meat from the shells. Don't forget to crack open the tails and claws and extract their meat, too.
- Toast the ciabattas under the grill. Once they're done, arrange the lettuce and watercress on the bottom half, top with the lobster meat and finish with a serving of tarragon mayonnaise.

CEVICHE OF BREAM

SERVES 4

Ceviche, a Latin American dish, is essentially raw fish soaked in a citrus marinade. Any white fish can be used, but firm varieties such as seabass and bream work best – though it's essential to buy the freshest bream you can from your local fishmonger for this dish and keep it chilled until you're ready to serve. Ceviche tastes lip-smackingly fresh and, best of all, it's super-simple to make – so easy, in fact, that you can involve kids in the preparation process. This is great as a starter, or served with bread and salad for lunch.

INGREDIENTS

4 fillets gilthead bream, scaled and pin-boned
2 spring onions, finely chopped
Handful mange tout, finely chopped
1 red chilli, finely chopped
1 lime, juiced

½ tsp fresh ginger, grated
100ml olive oil
25ml white wine vinegar
Handful coriander, chopped
2 lemons, cut into wedges

● We know we've said it already, but it bears repeating. Make sure you buy the freshest possible bream fillets to create this dish. Once you've got them, slice the fillets thinly and place into a bowl. Set aside.

● Place the spring onions and mange tout in a separate bowl, then add the chilli, lime juice, ginger, olive oil, white wine vinegar and half the coriander. Pour the mixture over the slices of bream and leave to marinate for around 10–15 minutes.

● Arrange the bream slices on a plate and pour over any marinade left in the bowl. Sprinkle with the rest of the coriander and serve with lemon wedges.

APPLE & MUSTARD SAUSAGE ROLLS

SERVES 4

Perfect for a picnic and great with a glass of wine or a beer, these straight-from-the-oven sausage rolls give off a delicious aroma, and as soon as we bring out a plateful for a group at The Hive, other customers start ordering them, too. Don't be tempted to scrimp on the ingredients. Use top-quality sausages from your local butcher (as herby and peppery as possible) and your favourite kind of eating apple – we think Braeburns work particularly well. Get them to the table quickly. A hot sausage roll is one of life's greatest pleasures.

INGREDIENTS

225g plain flour
100g butter, diced
1 egg
Milk

6–8 sausages, casing removed
Wholegrain mustard
1 firm eating apple, peeled and finely sliced

● First make the pastry. Sift the flour into a bowl, add the butter and rub it in with your fingertips until you have fine breadcrumbs. Stir in a pinch of sea salt and add 2–3 tbsp water to bind the pastry together. Knead the dough lightly on a floured surface, then wrap it in clingfilm and set aside in the fridge for at least 30 minutes.

● Preheat your oven to 180°C/350°F. Roll out the pastry on a floured surface until it has a thickness of around 3mm. Try to keep the shape as square as you can.

● Beat the egg together with a dash of milk then use the mixture to thinly coat the pastry.

● Cut the pastry into strips. These need to be the length of the sausages you'll be using and wide enough to fully wrap around them. The pastry will need to overlap a bit so you can seal the join.

● Spread a thin layer of mustard onto each strip.

● Lay a piece of apple onto each strip and place a sausage on top. Roll the pastry until it completely covers the filling. Gently press the pastry where it overlaps to seal the join.

● Cover a baking tray with greaseproof paper. Arrange the sausage rolls onto the tray and brush them with another coating of the egg-and-milk mixture.

● Bake in the oven for around 20 minutes until the sausage rolls are a golden-brown colour. Serve immediately while still hot.

FISH BAP WITH AÏOLI

MAKES 4 SANDWICHES

A fantastic, sustainable alternative to cod, gurnard is relatively inexpensive and its lean, firm white flesh is wonderfully tasty. Sandwiched inside a simple toasted white bap, the flavours of the fish, pancetta, peppery wild rocket and garlicky aïoli burst through – providing a huge whack of taste that kids will love just as much as adults. Gurnard can be bony, though, so do check the fillets thoroughly for those fiddly yet deceptively sharp spikes before serving to young children.

INGREDIENTS

3 egg yolks
2 cloves garlic
Few strands saffron
¼ tsp English mustard
½ lemon, juiced

150ml olive oil
4 slices pancetta
4 gurnard fillets, scaled and pin-boned
4 white baps, cut in half
Handful wild rocket

● First make the aïoli. Put the egg yolks, garlic, saffron, mustard and lemon juice into a food processor and blitz. Pour in the olive oil in a steady stream, blending continually, until the dressing reaches a thick consistency. Set aside.

● Preheat a hot grill and warm up a frying pan.

● Lay the pancetta out on a tray and grill until crisp. Set aside in a warm place.

● Oil and season the gurnard fillets, and place in the frying pan skin-side down. Don't turn until they're cooked two-thirds through (when the flesh is beginning to change from a translucent colour to a more solid one). Then turn down the heat and let them cook through slowly.

● Toast the baps under the grill. Once they're done, place a fish fillet in each one and top with wild rocket, a slice of pancetta (which you can cut into lardons if you prefer) and a spoonful of the aïoli.

THE CHESIL SMOKERY SALMON BOARD

SERVES 4

We're very lucky to have a wonderful smokery just a short drive away from The Hive. The Chesil Smokery on the edge of Bridport – which bills itself as 'the hottest little smokery in the west' – uses oak and apple wood chippings made from British trees to smoke everything from chicken, duck and venison to trout, mackerel and haddock. But it's the smoked salmon we particularly love. This simple recipe shows off its stunning flavour to perfection. If you haven't got a good smokery close to where you live, you can always place an order with our near-neighbour. Check out its website at www.chesilsmokery.com.

INGREDIENTS

1 cucumber
1 tbsp capers, chopped
Small bunch dill, chopped
60ml white wine vinegar
50g sugar

500g smoked salmon
Bunch wild rocket
Bunch watercress
Olive oil
1 lemon, cut into wedges

● Using a potato peeler, cut the cucumber into ribbons and place in a shallow bowl. Sprinkle with sea salt and set aside.

● Once you've let the cucumber stand for at least 15 minutes, rinse it in cold water and leave to dry.

● Place the chopped capers and dill into a bowl and pour in the white wine vinegar and sugar. Add the cucumber ribbons. At The Hive, we serve this 'pickle' mixture in a small glass kiln jar, but you can bring it to the table any way you like.

● Arrange the smoked salmon onto a board.

● Mix the wild rocket and watercress together then drizzle with a little olive oil. Add a squeeze of lemon then heap the salad onto the board.

● Serve with the pickle mixture and hunks of granary bread.

CRAYFISH, PRAWN & AVOCADO SALAD SANDWICH

MAKES 4 SANDWICHES

A perennial lunchtime favourite, our take on the classic 1980s prawn cocktail has proved to be incredibly popular with customers at The Hive. As ever, what makes this sandwich is the high quality of the ingredients. We use freshly baked granary bread from our own micro-bakery at West Bay, and prawns and crayfish from the day boats that bring their catch in from the waters just off Hive Beach. It's worth making your own mayonnaise, too; and as for the tomato ketchup? Well, we use Heinz naturally…

INGREDIENTS

Mayonnaise (see page 15)
Tomato ketchup
Small pinch smoked paprika
Dash Worcester sauce
1 lemon, juiced
400g cooked crayfish, peeled

400g cooked prawns, peeled
2 ripe avocados
Butter
8 slices granary bread
1 iceberg lettuce, chopped
Handful watercress

● Prepare your mayonnaise according to the instructions on page 15.
● Combine 4 tbsp of the mayonnaise with a small squirt of tomato ketchup, then add the smoked paprika, Worcester sauce and the juice of half a lemon. The sauce should taste creamy and sharp.
● Fold the crayfish and the prawns into the mayonnaise mixture. Set aside.
● Peel and slice the avocado, and squeeze the rest of the lemon juice over the slices to prevent them from turning brown.
● Butter the slices of granary bread, and pile the crayfish-and-prawn mixture onto 4 of them. Arrange the avocado slices, iceberg lettuce and watercress onto each before placing the final slice of buttered bread on top. Slice each sandwich in half and serve.

SASHIMI OF BEEF WITH TERIYAKI SAUCE

SERVES 4

The sweet, salty flavour of teriyaki sauce can be used to ramp up the flavour of salmon, tuna and chicken, but we think it's unbeatable served with sliced steak and a crunchy Asian salad.

INGREDIENTS

2 carrots, chopped finely into batons
Handful mange tout, finely sliced lengthways
Handful beansprouts
Small bunch spring onions, finely
sliced lengthways
1 red pepper, finely sliced into strips
2 red chillis, 1 finely diced and 1 finely
sliced lengthways
Olive oil

Large fillet steak
1 clove garlic, finely diced
1 small piece fresh ginger, finely diced
1 lime, zested and juiced
5 tbsp dark soy sauce
2 tbsp maple syrup
Handful coriander, chopped
Sesame seeds, to garnish

● Place all the vegetables and the finely diced red chilli in a bowl of iced water and set aside in the fridge. Preheat a frying pan over a high heat.

● Oil and season the steak. Seal the steak in the hot, dry frying pan until both sides have an even colour (30 seconds for each side should be enough). Make sure you seal around the edge of the steak as well. Remove from the pan and place on a dry cloth or paper towel for a minute or so.

● Wrap the steak tightly in clingfilm and put it in the freezer for around an hour.

● Now make the teriyaki sauce. Drizzle a little olive oil into a pan and fry the garlic, ginger and finely sliced chilli until lightly brown. Add the lime zest and juice, and pour in the soy sauce. Add the maple syrup and cook for a couple of minutes until the sauce begins to thicken, then turn down the heat and continue cooking slowly until it reaches a thick consistency.

● Take the steak from the freezer and remove the clingfilm. Using a very sharp knife, cut the meat finely into the thinnest slices you can.

● Take the vegetables from the fridge and drain them.

● Arrange the steak slices on a large plate then pile the crunchy vegetables on top. Drizzle over the warm teriyaki sauce and finish with a generous sprinkle of coriander and sesame seeds. Serve immediately.

SARDINE PÂTÉ SERVED WITH MELBA TOAST

SERVES 4

The humble sardine is a much-underrated fish. Maybe we've got so used to seeing it in tin cans that we've forgotten just how delicious it can be when served fresh. And as these beautiful, silvery fish are plentiful off the coast of Devon and Cornwall – which begins just the other side of Lyme Regis – we're always looking for new ways to serve them at The Hive. This wonderfully oily pâté goes perfectly with crisp slices of Melba toast and an ice-cold beer. Though you might want to lose one of those items if you're serving it up to kids.

INGREDIENTS

8 slices bread
16 sardine fillets, skinned and pin-boned
2 shallots, finely chopped
Pinch cayenne pepper
4 spring onions, finely chopped

70g butter
3 tsp olive oil
2 lemons; 1 juiced, 1 cut into wedges
2 sprigs flat-leaf parsley, chopped

● The Melba toast can be prepared up to a day in advance. To make it, toast the slices of bread and, once done, cut off all the crusts. Cut each slice in half lengthways, then make triangles of these halves. Place them on a baking tray and put them in an oven preheated to 180°C/350°F to colour and crisp up. Once cooked and cooled, seal them in an airtight container until you're ready to serve.
● When you're ready to prepare the pâté, preheat your oven to 180°C/350°F.
● Oil and season the sardine fillets, then place them on a baking tray and put them in the oven for around 5 minutes, until cooked through.
● Place the sardine fillets, shallots, cayenne pepper, spring onions, butter, olive oil and lemon juice into a food processor and blitz. Season to taste.
● Scoop out the pâté and put it into a bowl, then finish with a sprinkling of flat-leaf parsley and a lemon wedge. Serve with the Melba toast.

ASHLEY CHASE CHEESEBOARD WITH PINEAPPLE CHUTNEY

SERVES 4

The Hive is ideally placed for some of the best produce in the southwest and we're incredibly lucky to have Ford Farm, situated on the Ashley Chase estate, just up the road from us. The farm produces some wonderful local cheeses – and its oak-smoked Dorset Red, 15-month-aged Coastal Cheddar and Billie's Goat Cheddar have long been staples of the cheeseboards here at the café. It is possible to buy Ford Farm cheeses in some supermarkets, but it's probably easier to order them direct from www.fordfarm.com. This deliciously tangy chutney is the perfect accompaniment.

INGREDIENTS

1 large pineapple, roughly chopped

500g Bramley apples, peeled, cored and finely chopped

5cm piece fresh root ginger, finely chopped

1 red onion, finely chopped

140g dried figs, chopped

2 tsp black mustard seeds

½ tsp freshly grated nutmeg

500ml cider vinegar

400g light muscovado sugar

100g Dorset Red cheese

100g Coastal Cheddar cheese

100g Billie's Goat Cheddar cheese

● Put the pineapple pieces into a food processor and blitz until finely chopped.

● Tip the pineapple into a large saucepan along with the apples, ginger, onion, figs, spices, cider vinegar and 2 tsp sea salt.

● Bring to the boil, stirring constantly, then cook for 10 minutes or so until the apples have softened. Add the sugar and stir to dissolve. Simmer, stirring frequently, until the chutney has thickened. Be careful not to let the mixture burn and stick to the bottom of the pan.

● Pour the chutney into warm, sterilised jars and seal. It will keep for up to six months.

● Arrange the cheeses on a large, wooden board and serve with granary bread and a jar of chutney on the side.

SALMON SCOTCH EGGS

MAKES 4 EGGS

A staple of any good picnic lunch – especially when made at home – the Scotch egg is traditionally made with sausagement. Being somewhat fish-focused at The Hive, though, we couldn't help but experiment with a seafood version. And we've found that a combination of tender, pink salmon and its densely flavoured, smoked cousin – which we get from Bridport's Chesil Smokery – provides a fabulous twist on this British lunchtime classic. Try this recipe and you'll never be tempted to buy those tiny, tasteless versions from the supermarket picnic section ever again.

INGREDIENTS

6 eggs
Sunflower oil, for deep-frying
300g salmon fillets, skinned and pin-boned
200g smoked salmon
1 tsp capers

1 bunch dill
1 lime, juiced
Plain flour
150g breadcrumbs

● Bring a pan of water up to the boil and boil 4 of the eggs for 7 minutes, then remove them and put them straight into ice-cold water. Peel and set aside.

● Preheat the sunflower oil to 180°C/350°F in a large pan or deep-fat fryer.

● Blitz the salmon fillets, smoked salmon, capers, dill and lime juice, along with sea salt and freshly ground black pepper, in a food processor.

● Roll the hard-boiled eggs in the salmon mixture, ensuring each is completely covered.

● Whisk 2 more eggs together in a shallow bowl. Roll the covered eggs in flour, then in the egg mixture and, finally, in the breadcrumbs.

● Place the eggs into the pan or deep-fat fryer and cook for around 4–5 minutes, until golden-brown and crisp.

WEYMOUTH BROWN CRAB SANDWICH

MAKES 4 SANDWICHES

What's the point in dressing up a crab sandwich? This seaside treat, best enjoyed sitting beside the beach with a nice cup of tea, is at its best when it's utterly unadorned. At The Hive and The Watch House, we use Weymouth brown crab caught that day by fishermen just along the coast, and the quality of the meat is fantastic. To create the perfect sandwich, we've found that a mix of hand-picked white and brown meat served on freshly baked granary bread makes the most delicious combination, and a squeeze of lemon and a pinch of sea salt is all that's required to bring out the flavour.

INGREDIENTS

1 brown crab, to yield 170g white meat and 170g brown meat
Butter

8 slices granary bread
1 lemon, cut into wedges
4 handfuls salad leaves

● Prepare the crab according to the instructions on page 12 or, alternatively, ask your fishmonger to do it for you. Drop the white crab meat onto a metal tray to check if it still contains any shell.
● Butter the slices of granary bread.
● Mix the crab meat together, add a squeeze of lemon and season to taste with sea salt.
● Divide the crab meat between 4 sandwiches and cut each one into 4 triangles. Serve with lemon wedges and freshly dressed salad leaves on the side.

SWEET & SPICY NUTS

SERVES 4

A wonderful snack that's ideal to serve with pre-dinner drinks, these nuts, which take on the deliciously sweet flavours of honey and cinnamon as they cook, will keep in a jar for up to two months. If you can resist eating them straightaway (not as simple as it sounds), they make great presents for friends and relatives – especially when packed into a kiln jar that will release the fabulous aroma when popped open. This recipe is a great one to make with kids. After a little stirring and drizzling, there's not much more to do than tuck in.

INGREDIENTS

1 tsp ground cinnamon
½ tsp mixed spice
1 tbsp sunflower oil

400g mixed nuts (Brazils, almonds, cashews and macadamia)
2 tbsp honey

- Preheat your oven to 140°C/275°F.
- Stir the ground cinnamon and mixed spice into the sunflower oil. Add the nuts and mix until they're coated. Pour in 1 tbsp honey.
- Spread the nuts out onto a baking tray and cook in the oven for 10 minutes.
- Remove from the oven and drizzle the rest of the honey onto the nuts. Return to the oven and cook for a further 10 minutes.
- Allow the nuts to cool. Then either serve immediately or put them into sterilised jars to enjoy later.

BEACH CAFÉ COOKBOO

DORSET BLUE VINNEY, WALNUT & WILD ROCKET SANDWICH

MAKES 4 SANDWICHES

Thomas Hardy's favourite cheese, Dorset Blue Vinney has been made in the county for hundreds of years. Originally a by-product of the area's once-lucrative butter industry, the hard, crumbly cheese – which is made from skimmed milk – has a wonderfully tangy flavour that makes it an ideal accompaniment to salad. This sandwich, which looks as good as it tastes, combines the Blue Vinney with simply dressed peppery wild rocket and walnuts. The quality of the cheese is key to this dish, so it's worth seeking out the real stuff – which is traditionally made around Sturminster Newton.

INGREDIENTS

Butter
8 thick slices sourdough bread
Large wedge Dorset Blue Vinney cheese
Large handful walnuts

200g wild rocket
Olive oil
Balsamic vinegar

● Butter your sourdough slices and set aside.
● Crumble the Blue Vinney cheese into a bowl, and add the walnuts and wild rocket. Drizzle with a little olive oil and balsamic vinegar, and mix together.
● Arrange 4 sourdough slices on a serving dish and place a good handful of the Blue Vinney mixture on top of each. Top with the remaining sourdough slices and serve immediately.

SURF & TURF SANDWICH

MAKES 4 SANDWICHES

A staple of the US steakhouse, surf and turf – which refers to the dietary law-flouting combination of seafood and meat – may not be the most fashionable thing to order on our menu, but it is undeniably delicious. And, at the end of the day, that's all we really care about at The Hive. This sandwich version, in which wonderfully thin minute steaks share bread-space with tender, garlicky lobster tails, is the perfect lunchtime treat. We recommend you serve it with some homemade garlic mayonnaise on the side.

INGREDIENTS

Mayonnaise (see page 15)
2 cloves garlic, crushed
4 115g minute steaks
Butter

½ lemon, juiced
4 cooked lobster tails, meat removed
4 ciabattas, cut in half lengthways
1 iceberg lettuce, chopped

● Prepare your mayonnaise according to the instructions on page 15. Mix in one of the garlic cloves. Set aside in the fridge.
● Preheat a chargrill or a griddle pan over a high heat until it's smoking-hot and preheat your oven to 180°C/350°F.
● Cover each of the minute steaks in clingfilm and bash it with a meat mallet or rolling pin to tenderise.
● Combine the second garlic clove and a knob of butter, and add the lemon juice. Mix well then cover the lobster tails in the butter mixture before placing them on a baking tray and putting them in the oven. Cook until the butter has melted and the meat has warmed through.
● Toast the ciabattas under the grill and set aside in a warm place.
● Oil and season the minute steaks, and chargrill to your liking.
● Place a cooked minute steak in each ciabatta, add a lobster tail and top with iceberg lettuce. Serve immediately with the garlic mayonnaise on the side.

HOT-SMOKED SALMON WITH DILL CRÈME FRAÎCHE

SERVES 4

This incredibly simple recipe makes a perfect snack or starter. By 'hot-smoked salmon' we mean salmon that has been smoked in a smokery at around 80°C–120°C for a short period of time – a process that cooks it while adding a deliciously deep level of flavour to the tender flesh. And, while we get ours from The Chesil Smokery in nearby Bridport, it's worth finding out your local smokehouse as the supermarket-bought stuff just isn't the same.

INGREDIENTS

Bunch dill, chopped
100g crème fraîche
1 ½ lemons, cut into wedges
400g hot-smoked salmon

4 thick slices granary bread
200g watercress
Olive oil

● Combine the chopped dill with the crème fraîche and add the juice of half a lemon.

● Break the hot-smoked salmon into pieces and fold it into the crème fraîche mixture. Season to taste.

● Spoon the mixture onto the slices of granary bread and top each with a handful of watercress. Drizzle with a little olive oil and serve with lemon wedges.

STYLISH SUPPERS

GREY MULLET WITH ROASTED RED PEPPERS & CHORIZO

SERVES 4

A much-overlooked fish, grey mullet has a wonderfully earthy taste that goes incredibly well with the piquant flavours of chorizo and roasted red pepper. At The Hive, we get a lot of our grey mullet from the River Brit or the waters off West Bay, and it's worth asking your fishmonger where they source theirs from – the fish caught in estuaries or too close to the shore can have a rather muddy taste that can overwhelm a recipe. Get it right, though, and you'll create a delicious family meal you'll want to make again and again.

INGREDIENTS

4 red peppers, deseeded
Small pan new potatoes
4 grey mullet fillets
Olive oil

200g chorizo, sliced thickly
1 lemon, cut into wedges
Handful parsley, chopped

● Place the red peppers onto a grill or over a gas hob (or, as we do at The Hive, into a wood oven) and heat until the skin has blackened. When they've charred all over, remove the pepper from the heat, put it in a bowl and cover with clingfilm. Leave for 15 minutes then rub off the skin, before slicing the flesh into strips. Set aside.

● Boil the potatoes until soft and set aside in a warm place. Preheat a non-stick frying pan and season your grey mullet fillets.

● Drizzle a little olive oil into the frying pan, then put in the fillets skin-side down. Do not move for at least 3 minutes. Turn over and repeat on the other side. Take off the heat and leave to cook for a minute in the residual heat.

● While the fish is cooking, place the chorizo into another non-stick frying pan and gently heat until the oil begins to seep out.

● Add the cooked potatoes to the pan and work them with a fork until they've lightly broken up and have taken on the flavour of the chorizo. Add the roasted red pepper strips and roll through the mix. Season to taste.

● Divide the potato-and-chorizo mix between 4 bowls. Place a grey mullet fillet on top of each and finish with a squeeze of lemon and a sprinkling of chopped parsley.

CLAM & MUSSEL LINGUINE

SERVES 4

This hearty dish is the perfect family dinner. All children love pasta and the fun they'll have picking the meat from the mussels and clams, and mopping up the delicious creamy sauce with hunks of bread make this a real teatime treat. The good news is this recipe is incredibly simple to make and, so long as you use fresh shellfish (readily available from your local fishmonger) as opposed to the vacuum-packed variety sold in the supermarket, it's phenomenally tasty. Serve it up in a large bowl set in the middle of the table, add some pasta servers and watch everyone dig in.

INGREDIENTS

1 stick lemongrass, crushed
2 cloves garlic, chopped
750ml double cream
1kg mussels
1kg clams

500g linguine
Olive oil
1 large onion, diced
1 large glass white wine
1 bunch coriander, chopped

● Combine the lemongrass and garlic with the double cream and set aside for at least 1 hour to allow time for the flavours to infuse.
● Wash the mussels and clams in cold water and discard any that do not close when tapped.
● Bring a large saucepan of salted water up to the boil and add the linguine. Cook for 3–4 minutes if you're using fresh pasta; 15 minutes if you're using dried. Drain and set aside.
● Preheat a large frying pan or wok, and drizzle in a little olive oil. Add the onion and white wine, then put in the mussels and clams, and cover. Cook for 5 minutes or so, then pour in the lemongrass-and-garlic cream. Cook for another 8–10 minutes until the sauce has reduced and started to thicken, and the shellfish have opened.
● Discard any mussels and clams that remain closed. Season to taste.
● Add the drained linguine to the pan, then sprinkle in the coriander. Mix well and serve in a large bowl with hunks of fresh, crusty bread on the side.

WHOLE DOVER SOLE WITH LEMON BUTTER SAUCE

SERVES 4

Dover sole doesn't come cheap, but its distinctive sweet, mild flavour is ideally suited to the family dinner table. And, at The Hive, we like to serve it as simply as possible. This version, in which the roasted fish is accompanied by just a lemon butter sauce and a sprinkling of herbs, allows its wonderful taste to take centre-stage.

INGREDIENTS

4 medium Dover sole, top skin removed
Olive oil
700g green beans, ends removed
2 cloves garlic, chopped
1 shallot, finely chopped
60ml white wine

150ml double cream
60g butter
½ lemon, juiced
½ bunch chives, finely chopped
½ bunch dill, finely chopped

● Preheat your oven to 180°C/350°F.
● Place the Dover sole onto an oiled and seasoned baking tray. Season the fish and drizzle with olive oil, then bake for 10–15 minutes until cooked through.
● Bring a saucepan of salted water up to the boil and add the green beans. Blanch for 4–5 minutes, then remove and place in iced water to keep their colour and crispiness, and stop them from cooking further. Drain and set aside.
● Drizzle some olive oil into a saucepan and warm over a medium heat for at least 3 minutes. Add the garlic and shallot, and cook for 60 seconds. Then put in the green beans and cook for 3–5 minutes. Season to taste.
● To make the lemon butter sauce, pour the white wine into a saucepan and simmer over a medium heat for 4–5 minutes until it has reduced a little. Add the double cream and butter to the pan and continue cooking until it reaches a thick consistency. Stir in the lemon juice and remove from the heat.
● Divide the fish between 4 plates and pour over the lemon butter sauce. Finish with a sprinkling of chives and dill. Serve immediately with a large bowl of the sautéed beans.

TRAY-BAKED SALMON WITH OLIVES & TOMATOES

SERVES 4

Fabulously easy to make and equally impressive to look at – as well as eat – this delicious, one-tray combination of tender, pink salmon fillets, roasted cherry tomatoes and olives, and pungent herbs is sure to be a hit with your family. Get the basil, dill and parsley from your local greengrocer rather than from a packet, and ask your fishmonger for fresh wild salmon. You'll then be on your way to making this dish absolutely perfect.

INGREDIENTS

4 salmon fillets, scaled and pin-boned
Olive oil
Handful basil leaves, torn
Handful dill, chopped
Handful parsley, chopped
1 small punnet cherry tomatoes

Handful black olives, pitted
Handful green olives, pitted
2 cloves garlic, squashed
1 lemon, cut into wedges
1 red onion, roughly chopped

- Preheat your oven to 230°C/445°F.
- To get the salmon fillets nice and crispy, you will need to score the skin. With the skin-side up, roll the fillet slightly and make a cut around half an inch deep with a sharp knife. Don't cut completely across the skin. Score the skin several times in this way.
- Oil and season the salmon fillets. Arrange half of the basil, dill and parsley on a roasting tray and place the salmon on top. Roast in the oven for 10 minutes.
- Remove the tray from the oven and add the cherry tomatoes, olives, garlic, lemon wedges, red onion and the rest of the herbs. Season with sea salt and freshly ground black pepper, and drizzle with olive oil.
- Return to the oven and roast for another 10 minutes or so until the salmon has cooked.
- Serve immediately with new potatoes, crème fraîche and watercress.

GRILLED FILLET OF COLEY WITH SMOKED GARLIC MASH

SERVES 4

Coley is an inexpensive and sustainable alternative to cod, and it's every bit as versatile. This simple presentation – brushed with fennel oil and accompanied by deliciously smoky garlic mash and fennel slices – makes for a seriously impressive family meal.

INGREDIENTS

2 bulbs fennel
Olive oil
800g potatoes, peeled and quartered
Butter

1 bulb smoked garlic
4 225g coley fillets, scaled and pin-boned
Handful wild rocket

- Preheat your oven to 180°C/350°F.
- Slice the fennel bulbs lengthways into inch-thick pieces, then place in an oven dish and drizzle generously with olive oil. Cook in the oven for around 45 minutes until soft. Pour the fennel oil into a bowl and retain. Set the fennel strips aside.
- Boil the potatoes until soft then drain. Leave for a couple of minutes then add a knob of butter and mash until light and fluffy.
- Crush the smoked-garlic bulb and add it to the mashed potato, a little bit at a time. Keep tasting the mash and stop when you achieve the desired flavour. Set aside in a warm place.
- Preheat a hot grill.
- To get the coley fillets nice and crispy, you will need to score the skin. With the skin-side up, roll the fillet slightly and make a cut around half an inch deep with a sharp knife. Don't cut completely across the skin. Score the skin several times in this way.
- Oil the coley fillets with the fennel oil and season to taste. Place them on a baking tray and grill until the skin is crispy and the fish has cooked through.
- Put a large spoonful of the smoked-garlic mash onto each of 4 plates and top with a few slices of fennel and some wild rocket. Arrange a coley fillet on top and serve immediately.

BAKED GILTHEAD BREAM WITH HERBS & GARLIC

SERVES 4

With its fine, delicate flavour, the gilthead bream – which hails from the warmer waters of southern Europe – can be relied upon to provide a Mediterranean taste to brighten up even the gloomiest West Dorset afternoon – especially when baked in this fashion with plenty of herbs and garlic. Its bright, silvery skin and pinkish flesh are aesthetically pleasing, too, which is a bonus when you're attempting to impress dinner-party guests. Though the delicious aroma of this dish as it cooks in the oven is sure to do that anyway.

INGREDIENTS

8 sprigs rosemary

8 sprigs thyme

8 cloves garlic, finely chopped

8 bay leaves

4 whole gilthead bream, gutted and scaled

Olive oil

Bunch parsley, chopped

1 lemon, cut into wedges

● Preheat your oven to 180°C/350°F.

● Stuff 2 springs of rosemary, 2 sprigs of thyme, a clove of garlic and a bay leaf into each of the gilthead bream. Arrange on a baking tray, drizzle with olive oil, and season with sea salt and freshly ground black pepper. Bake in the oven for 10 minutes.

● Remove the fish from the oven and scatter with the remaining bay leaves and garlic. Drizzle with more olive oil then bake for a further 10 minutes until cooked through.

● Divide the gilthead bream between 4 plates and scatter with the parsley. Serve immediately with lemon wedges on the side.

SEABASS WITH SORREL SAUCE & CRISPY NEW POTATOES

SERVES 4

The slightly sour, almost lemony taste of sorrel goes brilliantly with the firm texture and mild flavour of seabass. We like to use wild sorrel in this recipe – and not just because it grows plentifully in West Dorset at certain times of the year. We find its tanginess works perfectly in this dish, and it's always a joy when we spot its distinctive leaves growing in the woodland around us. Though many people would frown at the idea of giving a rich sauce containing vermouth to children, we assure you the alcohol all burns off during the cooking process. Kids with more adventurous palates will love this.

INGREDIENTS

800g new potatoes, cut in half
1 shallot, finely chopped
400ml fish stock (see page 15)
150ml vermouth or dry white wine
250ml double cream
½ lemon, juiced

Bunch sorrel leaves, torn
Butter
Olive oil
4 400–500g seabass fillets, scaled
and pin-boned

● Bring a pan of salted water up to the boil, then add the new potatoes. They are cooked when you insert a thin knife into them and they slip off easily. Set aside.
● To make the sauce, put the shallot in a pan with the fish stock and the vermouth. Bring to the boil and reduce by half, then add the cream and lemon juice, and season to taste. At the last minute, throw in the sorrel. Remove from the heat and set aside.
● Melt a knob of butter in a frying pan and drizzle in a little olive oil. Add the new potatoes and cook until crispy and golden-brown.
● Heat some olive oil in a non-stick frying pan. Place the seabass fillets into the pan, skin-side down, and sear for 3–4 minutes. Season the top of each fillet then flip and cook the other side for a few seconds over a medium heat.
● To serve, divide the sorrel sauce between 4 plates and place a seabass fillet on top of each. Spoon some crispy new potatoes onto the side.

FISH & SAFFRON STEW

SERVES 4

Though it will undoubtedly be the delicious chunks of monkfish and seabass, and all the juicy king prawns that'll take the plaudits in this dish, the real credit here goes to the icky bits – the fishbones and shells – that intensify over time create the wonderful flavours in the stock base. Not that your kids need to see them, of course. You'll strain them out long before any child has chance to turn up their nose and say 'yuck'. And they certainly won't argue with this deep, dense, warming stew when you place it – still sumptuously steaming – into the middle of the dinner table.

INGREDIENTS

1 small monkfish

1 small seabass

500g king prawns

Handful mussels

1 bulb garlic, outer layers removed

1 carrot, roughly chopped

2 leeks, roughly chopped

1 fennel head

1 onion, roughly chopped

3–4 ripe tomatoes, quartered

Pinch saffron

1 sprig thyme

1 bay leaf

1 tsp fennel seeds

Handful coriander leaves, chopped

● Fillet the monkfish and seabass according to the instructions on page 11 or, alternatively, ask your fishmonger to do it for you. Make sure you reserve the fishbones.

● Dice the monkfish and seabass meat into chunks, and set aside. Then peel the prawns – reserving the shells.

● Wash the mussels in cold water and discard any that do not close when tapped.

● To make a stock, place the fishbones and prawn shells in a large saucepan and gently heat it to release the flavours. Next, throw in the garlic, carrot, leeks, fennel, onion and mussels; then add the tomatoes, saffron, thyme, bay leaf and fennel seeds. Cook until softened and then cover with water.

● Bring the stock up to a gentle simmer (without letting it boil) and cook for around 30 minutes. Once all the flavours have had time to intensify, strain the stock and return to the heat. Reduce by half.

● Just before serving, add the diced monkfish and seabass to the stock and let it cook for a couple of minutes. Divide between 4 bowls and finish each with a sprinkle of coriander.

GRILLED FILLET OF COD WITH SPINACH & BUTTER SAUCE

SERVES 4

If your children have only ever eaten cod encased in batter and served with a portion of salt-and-vinegary chips, this recipe is sure to open their eyes to the potential of this delicious fish. There are few things more delightful to come out of the sea than a snow-white fillet of firm, fresh cod, simply cooked and accompanied by a rich, tasty sauce. And this version, served with a pile of dark-green, buttery spinach, is as much a feast for the eyes as it is for the palate.

INGREDIENTS

200ml fish stock (see page 15)
100ml white wine
100ml white wine vinegar
2 shallots, finely diced
250g butter, finely diced

Small bunch chives, chopped
Olive oil
4 225g cod fillets, scaled and pin-boned
250g spinach, washed
Extra butter, to wilt the spinach

● Preheat a hot grill.
● Pour the fish stock into a saucepan and add the white wine, white wine vinegar and shallots. Bring to a boil and cook until the liquid has reduced by two-thirds, then turn down the heat and slowly whisk in the butter.
● Remove from the heat and mix in the chives. Set aside in a warm place.
● Oil and season the cod fillets. Place them on a baking tray and grill until the skin is crispy and the fish has cooked through. Set aside in a warm place.
● Preheat a frying pan over a high heat. Put the spinach in the pan, add a knob of butter and season to taste. Cook for a couple of minutes, stirring occasionally, until the spinach has wilted.
● Divide the spinach between 4 bowls. Add a cod fillet to each and drizzle with the butter sauce. Serve while still hot.

SEABASS FILLET WITH MANGO & CHILLI SALSA

SERVES 4

The seabass we serve at The Hive are line-caught by local fisherman Brett Hibbitt, who lifts them from the turbulent waters of The Race off Portland Bill and brings them into the café within a couple of hours of them leaving the sea. But if you can't get seabass as quickly as this, try to obtain fish that's as fresh as possible. Just ask your fishmonger for the most recent catch. The firm texture and delicate flavour of the fish complements the sharp and fruity salsa in this recipe wonderfully. We recommend serving it with a crisp green salad and some sautéed new potatoes.

INGREDIENTS

2 ripe mangos, peeled and deseeded
1 red chilli, finely chopped
1 red onion, diced
Small bunch chives, chopped

2 limes, zested and juiced
Olive oil
4 wild seabass fillets, pin-boned

● First, prepare your salsa. Dice the flesh of the mangos into small pieces and place into a bowl, then add the red chilli, red onion, chives, and the lime zest and juice. Season with sea salt and freshly ground black pepper, and set aside.
● Preheat a non-stick frying pan. Oil and season the seabass fillets, and place them skin-side down in the pan. Don't turn until they're cooked two-thirds through (when the flesh is beginning to change from a translucent colour to a more solid one). Then turn down the heat and let them cook through slowly.
● Take 4 plates and place a seabass fillet on each. Serve immediately with the mango and chilli salsa.

SPECIAL OCCASIONS

SQUID WITH ROASTED RED PEPPERS & OLIVES

SERVES 4

Though loved in the Mediterranean, squid is often overlooked by British seafood-eaters – which is a shame. Inexpensive and readily available, it makes a memorable, flavoursome lunch or supper the whole family will savour. And while the crisp, golden rings of calamari will always be a favourite, squid is also delicious in stews – and this dish's two-hour cooking time makes the flesh exquisitely tender. Leave out the chillies if you're serving this to young children.

INGREDIENTS

3 red peppers
1 large squid
3 red onions, roughly chopped
1 clove garlic, crushed
2 bird's eye chillies, finely chopped
Olive oil

1 tbsp paprika
Pinch saffron
1 punnet cherry tomatoes
Handful black olives, pitted
1 lime, cut into wedges
Handful parsley, chopped

● Preheat your oven to 200°C/400°F.
● Place the red peppers onto a grill or over a gas hob (or, as we do at The Hive, into a wood oven) and heat until the skin has blackened. When it's charred all over, remove the pepper from the heat, put it in a bowl and cover with clingfilm. Leave for 15 minutes then rub off the skin, before slicing the flesh into strips. Set aside.
● Prepare the squid according to the instructions on page 12 or, alternatively, ask your fishmonger to do it for you. Cut it into thin rings.
● Sweat the red onions, garlic and chillies with a little olive oil in a sauté pan until soft.
● Add the squid rings and fry for a few minutes, then add the paprika, saffron, sliced red peppers and cherry tomatoes, and cover with water. Bring up to the boil, then turn down the heat, cover with a lid and place in the oven for around two hours until the squid is tender.
● Divide between 4 bowls and garnish each with the olives. Finish with a squeeze of lime and a sprinkle of parsley. Serve immediately with crusty bread.

CHARGRILLED LOBSTER WITH HERB BUTTER

SERVES 4

The vast majority of the lobsters we serve at The Hive and The Watch House are caught by local fisherman Steve Elsworth, who gets them from the stretch of sea between Hive Beach and Golden Cap. As we see Steve almost every day, the lobsters we serve are as fresh as they come. Forget food miles; most of the time we're talking food yards. The taste of the lobster meat, obviously, is stunning; and, when it comes to serving it up to our customers, we prefer to keep things very simple. This delicious butter simply complements its flavour.

INGREDIENTS

1 bunch parsley, chopped
1 bunch chives, chopped
1 bunch dill, chopped

1 lemon, juiced and zested
250g butter
4 cooked lobsters

● Preheat a chargrill or a griddle pan over a high heat until it's smoking-hot.
● To make the herb butter, combine the parsley, chives, dill, lemon juice and zest with the butter and mix well.
● Halve the lobsters according to the instructions on page 13 or, alternatively, ask your fishmonger to do it for you.
● Spoon the herb butter over the white lobster meat then place each halved lobster onto the chargrill, flesh-side down. Remove the lobsters after a few minutes and spoon on more herb butter before replacing.
● Cook for another minute or so, until the lobster meat has warmed through.
● Spoon some more herb butter onto the hot meat and serve immediately with a crisp, green salad and some crusty bread.

PAN-FRIED SCALLOPS WITH TRUFFLE MASH & CRISPY PANCETTA

SERVES 4

Wholesome and hearty, with more than a hint of luxury provided by the dash of truffle oil in the mashed potato, this dish makes a fulsome family feast. The saltiness of the pancetta is the perfect contrast to the delicacy of the scallops. Enjoy.

INGREDIENTS

4 large potatoes, peeled
8 slices pancetta
1 clove garlic, crushed
200g butter
Truffle oil

Double cream
Olive oil
16 scallops
½ lemon, juiced
Handful wild rocket

● Boil the potatoes until soft then drain. Leave for a couple of minutes then mash until light and fluffy. Set aside in a warm place.
● Preheat a hot grill.
● Lay the pancetta slices out on a tray and grill until crisp. Set aside in a warm place.
● Combine the garlic with 150g butter and set aside.
● Preheat two heavy-bottomed frying pans – one of which needs to be very hot. Put the mashed potato into the cooler pan with a knob of butter, a drizzle of truffle oil and a splash of double cream. Keep stirring the mash until it's piping-hot, then turn the heat right down and season to taste.
● Oil and season the scallops, then place them into the other hot frying pan. Arrange them in a clockwise direction, remembering your starting point. After around 90 seconds, turn the scallops over in the same order.
● Add the garlic butter and the lemon juice to the scallops pan. Remove the pan from the heat as soon as the butter has melted.
● Place the truffle mash in a large serving bowl, arrange the scallops on top and finish with wild rocket and the pancetta slices. Drizzle over the pan juices and serve immediately.

ROASTED SEABASS WITH ROSEMARY & CONFIT LEMONS

SERVES 4

There's something undeniably impressive about a seabass. It's a beautiful fish, sure enough, and its fine, subtle flavour means it works just as well cooked simply or dressed up with other ingredients. We get almost all our seabass from the turbulent waters of The Race off Portland Bill, where they're line-caught and brought to us within a couple of hours. And it's worth sourcing the wild variety for your own table. There's nothing wrong with the farmed variety per se; it's just that the free-range variety tastes so much better.

INGREDIENTS

4 lemons, sliced
Olive oil
½ bunch rosemary
1 1–2kg wild seabass

1 orange, zested
2 tsp fennel seeds
1 red chilli, finely sliced
Wild rocket

● Preheat your oven to 180°C/350°F.
● Put the lemon slices into a pan and drizzle generously with olive oil. Add the rosemary and cook over a low heat for 15 minutes or so until soft. Remove from the heat and set aside.
● Stuff the seabass with the cooked rosemary and half the lemons. Use the oil from the pan to oil the fish, and season it with the orange zest, fennel seeds, chilli and sea salt. Put the fish on a roasting tray and roast in the oven for 40 minutes or so until cooked through.
● Place the seabass on a large board or platter and arrange the rest of the lemons and rosemary on top. Finish with a handful of wild rocket and a drizzle of lemon-and-rosemary oil. Serve immediately.

WILD HALIBUT WITH SAMPHIRE & LOBSTER BUTTER

SERVES 4

The halibut is a very big fish indeed. They regularly weigh in at around the 50kg mark and we've had ones delivered to The Hive that have fed more than 150 people. We're not suggesting you buy a whole one to make this dish – unless you and your family have got very big appetites – but it's worth getting hold of decent-sized portions for this recipe, as the firm, clean-tasting meat is excellent with the juicier flesh of fresh lobster and the indulgent flavour of garlic butter. This dish goes really well with sautéed new potatoes.

INGREDIENTS

1 lobster
1 clove garlic, crushed
Handful chives, chopped
200g butter
Olive oil

4 225g wild halibut fillets, scaled
and pin-boned
100g samphire
½ lemon, juiced
Handful wild rocket

● Prepare the lobster according to the instructions on page 13. Preheat a hot grill.
● Cut the lobster in half lengthways. Crack the claws and cut the tails open with scissors. Extract the meat from the lobster and, along with the tail and claw meat, chop it into chunks and place in a large bowl. Set aside in the fridge.
● Combine the garlic and the chives with the butter. Set aside. Preheat a hot grill.
● Oil and season the wild halibut fillets. Place them on a baking tray and grill until the skin is golden-brown and the fish has cooked through. Set aside in a warm place.
● In a warm pan, sauté the samphire for a minute or two. Add the lobster meat, garlic butter and the lemon juice. Cook until the butter has melted and the meat has warmed through.
● Divide the wild halibut fillets between 4 bowls. Add a spoonful of samphire and lobster butter to each. Arrange some wild rocket on the side and serve immediately.

HOT SHELLFISH IN A WOOD SORREL DRESSING

SERVES 4

This dish is a combination of all ingredients that can be found within walking distance of The Hive and The Watch House. It's well-known we have some of the best-tasting shellfish in the UK living in the waters off the Dorset coast, but did you know about the wonderfully sour, slightly lemony wood sorrel that grows abundantly all around the coastline? If you can't get hold of wood sorrel, simply substitute it with spinach in a little lemon juice. This dish may look complicated but it couldn't be easier to prepare.

INGREDIENTS

Handful wood sorrel, chopped

2 tbsp white wine vinegar

1 lemon, juiced

Olive oil

1 cooked lobster

1 cooked brown crab

500g mussels

12 scallops

12 king prawns in their shells

Butter

1 clove garlic, crushed

1 glass white wine

● First, make the dressing. Combine the wood sorrel with the white wine vinegar, lemon juice and a drizzle of olive oil. Season with sea salt and freshly ground black pepper and set aside.

● Prepare the lobster and crab according to the instructions on pages 12 and 13 or, alternatively, ask your fishmonger to extract the meat for you.

● Wash the mussels in cold water and discard any that do not close when tapped.

● Preheat a large frying pan. Once hot, drizzle in a little olive oil.

● Put the lobster, crab, mussels, scallops and king prawns into the pan and cook for 2 minutes. Then add a knob of butter, the garlic and white wine, and continue cooking until everything has warmed through and the mussels have opened. Discard any mussels that remain closed.

● Divide the shellfish between 4 bowls and drizzle over the wood sorrel dressing. Serve immediately with a crisp, green salad.

LARGE TURBOT WITH A LIGHT FISH SAUCE

SERVES 4

The fine, distinctive taste of turbot has earned it the title of King of the Flatfish, and this recipe shows it off in its simplest form: oven-roasted with a light sauce made from white wine and fish stock on the side. There's little point in dressing up something so flavoursome with ingredients that aren't fit to share the same plate. Seriously impressive, this dish will wow any dinner-party guests as well as garnering you admiring looks should you serve it up to your family.

INGREDIENTS

Olive oil
1 1–2kg turbot
2 shallots, finely chopped
100ml fish stock (see page 15)

Glass white wine
Double cream
Butter
1 bunch chervil, chopped

- Preheat your oven to 180°C/350°F.
- Oil and season the turbot, and place on a roasting tray. Put it into the oven and roast for 30 minutes. Check the fish is cooked. It should feel firm when you press it.
- While the turbot is cooking, make the light fish sauce. Put the shallots and white wine into a saucepan over a high heat and reduce until almost all the wine has evaporated.
- Pour in the fish stock and reduce by two thirds, then add a splash of double cream. Allow the sauce to reduce a little then lower the heat and add a knob of butter. Whisk, remove from the heat and add the chervil. Season to taste and set aside in a warm place.
- Place the turbot on a large serving dish and serve immediately with a jug of the light fish sauce on the side.

STICKY KING PRAWNS

SERVES 4

A dish containing king prawns is always going to impress. There's something about the sheer size of these crustaceans and the juicy, lobster-like flavour of their flesh that appeals to everyone. At The Hive, we always cook the king prawns in their shell because of the added flavour it provides, but if you're making this dish for children or those who find the whole peeling process too fiddly, you can always remove them before you start.

INGREDIENTS

2 cloves garlic, crushed
100g butter
32 king prawns in their shells
Olive oil
Pinch smoked paprika

Small piece fresh ginger, grated
Bottle sweet chilli sauce
2 lemons, cut into wedges
Handful coriander, roughly chopped

● Preheat a frying pan. Combine the garlic with the butter.
● Put the king prawns into the hot pan along with the garlic butter and a drizzle of olive oil. Cook for 1 minute.
● Add the smoked paprika and grated ginger, and cook for a further 2 minutes, then pour in the sweet chilli sauce and the juice of 1 lemon. Continue cooking until the prawns are opaque and have cooked through.
● Arrange the sticky king prawns in a large serving bowl, then finish with a sprinkle of coriander and lemon wedges. Drizzle with the pan juices then serve immediately with crusty granary bread and a green salad.

TRIO OF RED MULLET, GREY MULLET & JOHN DORY

SERVES 4

Three delicious fish, served with a bowlful of chargrilled roasted vegetables. Lovely.

INGREDIENTS

2 sweet potatoes cut into 3cm cubes

2 red onions, cut into thin wedges

Olive oil

2 large potatoes, cut into 3cm cubes

1–2 aubergines, sliced thinly

3 courgettes, sliced thinly lengthways

2 vines cherry tomatoes

Balsamic vinegar

3 lemons, cut into wedges

Pinch oregano

Handful sun-dried tomatoes

Handful black olives, pitted

Bunch parsley, chopped

2 400–500g red mullet, scaled and gutted

1 500–750g grey mullet, scaled and gutted

1 500-750g John Dory, scaled and gutted

4 sprigs rosemary

Small handful basil leaves

● Preheat a chargrill or a griddle pan until smoking-hot. Preheat your oven to 180°C/350°F.

● Place the sweet potatoes and red onions into a roasting dish and drizzle with olive oil. Put into the oven for 15 minutes or so.

● Put the potatoes into the chargrill and char on a couple of sides. Then remove and char the aubergines and courgettes on both sides. Add all to the roasting dish and top with the cherry tomatoes. Drizzle with a little balsamic vinegar and a squeeze of lemon juice, and sprinkle on the oregano. Return to the oven and roast for another 10 minutes.

● To make the dressing, put the sun-dried tomatoes, olives and half the parsley into a food processor with 100ml olive oil, a squeeze of lemon and a sprinkle of sea salt. Blitz and set aside.

● Turn the oven up to 220°C/425°F. Place the fish onto a roasting tray and season. Put a lemon wedge and sprig of rosemary inside each fish, and cook for 8–10 minutes.

● Arrange the fish on a large board, scatter over a few of the chargrilled vegetables and spoon the sun-dried tomato-and-olive dressing over the top. Sprinkle over the rest of the parsley and basil, and serve with lemon wedges on the side. Accompany with a large bowlful of the chargrilled vegetables.

TURBOT STEAK WITH PANCETTA & CAVA CREAM SAUCE

SERVES 4

Known for its rich taste and subtle texture, turbot is ideal for a celebratory meal. And when it's served in this rich cava cream sauce, infused with the sharpness of freshly grated Parmesan, it makes a real treat. At The Hive, we get much of our turbot from Weymouth fisherman Brett Hibbit, who line-catches them in the Race off Portland Bill. But if you ask your fishmonger for the freshest fish available, then your recreation of this dish should taste just as good.

INGREDIENTS

400g sprouts
Butter
1 shallot, finely diced
250g pancetta lardons
125ml cava

100ml fish stock (see page 15)
75ml double cream
50g Parmesan, grated
4 400g turbot steaks, skin left on
Olive oil

● Preheat your oven to 220°C/425°F.
● Bring a saucepan of salted water up to the boil and add the sprouts. Blanch for 2–3 minutes, then remove and place in cold water to cool and stop them from cooking further. Drain and set aside.
● To make the sauce, melt a knob of butter in a saucepan and sweat the shallot for a couple of minutes. Add the pancetta and cook for another minute, then pour in the cava and fish stock and reduce by three-quarters. Pour in the cream and bring to the boil, then stir in the Parmesan. Add the sprouts and shred. Remove from the heat and set aside in a warm place.
● Place the turbot steaks, skin-side up, onto an oiled and seasoned roasting tray. Season the fish and drizzle with olive oil, then roast for 10–15 minutes until cooked through.
● Put the sauce back onto the heat to warm through, then divide between 4 plates. Arrange the turbot steaks on top of each and serve immediately.

WHOLE ROASTED HALIBUT WITH PAN-FRIED SCALLOPS

SERVES 4

The halibut is the largest flatfish to swim in the waters off the Dorset coast and can grow to lengths of more than four metres. We're not suggesting you ask your fishmonger for one that big – unless, of course, you've got a giant oven. A fish of a kilo or two should be more than enough for you and your family to sample its exquisitely meaty flavour. This recipe can also be made with halibut steaks, but for maximum visual effect we recommend serving it whole.

INGREDIENTS

Olive oil
1 1–2kg whole halibut (see page 11)
12 scallops
200g samphire
4 tbsp capers

1 clove garlic, crushed
White wine
Butter
1 lemon, juiced
Small bunch parsley, chopped

- Preheat your oven to 180°C/350°F.
- Oil and season the halibut, and place it onto a baking tray. Put it into the oven and bake for 30–40 minutes.
- Once the fish has cooked, turn off the oven. Leave the fish inside to rest and keep warm in the residual heat. Warm a large frying pan over a high heat.
- Season the scallops with sea salt and olive oil, and place them into the hot frying pan. Turn each scallop after 45–60 seconds (depending on their size). Make sure the scallops are golden-brown where they've been in contact with pan, and have an even colour on both sides.
- Add the samphire, capers and garlic to the pan, then pour in a splash of white wine. Once the wine has reduced a little, add a knob of butter, the lemon juice and the parsley.
- Place the halibut on a large platter, arrange the scallops on top and pour the sauce over both. Serve immediately.

SURF & TURF

SERVES 4

The ultimate all-American platter, this combination of Parmesan-sprinkled lobster thermidor and pan-fried fillet steak works just as well down here on Hive Beach as it does in the coves on the other side of the Atlantic. We have some wonderful beef suppliers within a few miles of the café and the lobsters we use are lifted daily from the water just a few metres from our kitchen, so we're guaranteed absolute freshness and superb flavour. This is an excellent meal for a birthday supper or other celebration.

INGREDIENTS

4 225g fillet steaks
2 lobsters
2 shallots, diced
White wine vinegar
100ml fish stock (see page 15)
50ml double cream

2 tsp English mustard
50g strong cheddar
2 egg yolks
Parmesan
Olive oil
2 handfuls wild rocket

● Bring the steaks up to room temperature. Prepare your lobsters according to the instructions on page 13 or, alternatively, ask your fishmonger to do it for you.
● To make the thermidor sauce, put the shallots in a pan with a splash of white wine vinegar and reduce by half.
● Add the fish stock and reduce the mixture until almost all of the liquid has evaporated, then put in two thirds of the cream and reduce once again. Add in the mustard and cheddar and leave to cool.
● Cut the cooled lobster in half and remove the tail and claw meat. Retain the shells and chop the meat into chunks.
● Whisk the egg yolks and add to the thermidor sauce. Then whisk up the remaining cream and stir that in as well. Mix in the chopped lobster.
● Spoon the thermidor mixture back into the lobster shells and grate parmesan over the top.
● Preheat a frying pan over a high heat and warm up the grill. Oil and season the fillet steaks and fry for 3 minutes each side (for medium).
● Allow the steaks to rest for 5 minutes, so the juices have time to reabsorb. Meanwhile, grill the lobsters until they're golden-brown and hot throughout.
● Divide the steaks and lobsters between 4 plates, place wild rocket on the side and serve.

SEABASS EN PAPILLOTE WITH THAI FLAVOURS

SERVES 4

'En papillote', which translates literally as 'in parchment', is a French cooking technique in which meat or fish is cooked in a parcel to prevent moisture – and flavour – from escaping. It lends itself particularly well to the delicate taste of seabass, especially when it's teamed with the zingy flavours of Thai cuisine. And it's pretty theatrical, too. Open up the parcel to release the delicious aroma of the ginger, lime, coriander and chilli, and you'll have won over your dinner guests before they've even picked up their forks.

INGREDIENTS

2 1kg seabass, filleted, scaled and pin-boned
2 pak choi, cut in half lengthways
Handful coriander, chopped
Handful Thai basil leaves, chopped
2 red chillies, finely sliced
1 thumb-sized piece ginger, grated

4 stalks lemongrass
White wine vinegar
Soy sauce
1 lime, cut into wedges
Sesame oil

- Preheat your oven to 180°C/350°F.
- Get 4 sheets of greaseproof paper ready. These need to be at least twice the size of the seabass fillets.
- Place a piece of pak choi onto each sheet of paper, and top with coriander and Thai basil leaves. Put a seabass fillet on top of each parcel and divide the chilli, ginger and lemongrass evenly between them.
- Roll up the sides of the greaseproof paper to create 4 open parcels, then add a splash of white wine vinegar and soy sauce, a squeeze of lime and a drizzle of sesame oil to each.
- Fold the paper at the top to seal the parcels and place on a baking tray. Bake in the oven for 15 minutes or so until the seabass is cooked through.
- Serve in the parcels with rice or a crunchy Thai salad.

STARGAZY PIE

SERVES 4

A traditional Cornish dish of baked pilchards with eggs and West Country cider, this delicious pie is something of a hard sell when it comes to younger children, who may well baulk at the idea of eating something with real fish heads poking out of the top. But older kids – and anyone with fond memories of Desperate Dan and his cow pies from *The Dandy* – will absolutely love it. The Cornish version is always made with pilchards, as they're so plentiful off the coast of the peninsula, but feel free to make this pie with mackerel or sardines instead. Both work equally well.

INGREDIENTS

6 tbsp fresh white breadcrumbs

150ml milk

2 tbsp fresh parsley, chopped

1 medium onion, chopped

1 lemon, zested and juiced

6 pilchards, heads left on

2 hard-boiled eggs, chopped

2 rashers lean bacon, chopped

150ml dry cider

225g shortcrust or puff pastry

● Preheat your oven to 220°C/425°F.

● Soak the breadcrumbs in the milk and leave them to swell a little. Then add the parsley, onion, lemon zest and 3 tbsp lemon juice. Mix well.

● Prepare the pilchards according to the instructions on page 11 or, alternatively, ask your fishmonger to do it for you. Make sure you leave the heads on.

● Divide the stuffing mixture between the pilchards and fill them generously. Fold them then arrange into a round ovenproof dish, with the tails pointing downwards and the heads resting on the edge.

● Arrange the eggs, bacon and cider around and in between the pilchards. Season with sea salt and freshly ground black pepper.

● Roll the pastry out to the size of the dish onto a cold surface sprinkled with flour to prevent it from sticking. Press it onto the top of the dish, leaving the pilchard heads exposed around the rim.

● Bake the pie in the oven for 15 minutes, then reduce the heat to 190°C/375°F and bake for a further 25 minutes.

● Remove from the oven and cool for a few minutes, then serve in the dish.

PIZZAS

CHORIZO & ROASTED RED PEPPER PIZZA

MAKES 2 PIZZAS

Chorizo, chilli and red pepper give a huge hit of flavour to this delicious, Spanish-inspired pizza. Buy the best chorizo you can afford and slice it thinly so it blends perfectly with the melted cheese and caramelised onion. We recommend finishing with a scattering of red chilli – that way, you're guaranteed a hot burst of flavour with every slice, and those who aren't chilli fans can simply pick them off. The final touch – a handful of rocket added to the centre of the pizza before serving – offsets the smouldering heat to perfection. Younger children will enjoy the chorizo and roasted pepper, but leave the chilli for the grown-ups.

INGREDIENTS

1 red pepper
Pizza dough (see page 17)
Tomato sauce (see page 17)
2 chorizo, cooked, cooled and thinly sliced
½ red onion, thinly sliced

70g mozzarella, sliced
30g cheddar, grated
1 red chilli, finely sliced
50g rocket, washed

● Preheat your oven to 200°C/400°F. If you're using a wood oven, bring it up to 400°C/800°F.
● Place the red pepper onto a grill or over a gas hob (or, as we do at The Hive, into a wood oven) and heat until the skin has blackened. When it's charred all over, remove the pepper from the heat, put it in a bowl and cover with clingfilm. Leave for 15 minutes then rub off the skin, before slicing the flesh into strips. Set aside.
● Roll the pizza dough out onto a cold surface sprinkled with semolina to prevent it from sticking. Create two pizza bases by rolling the dough out as thinly as possible (this ensures crispiness).
● Spread the tomato sauce, chorizo, red onion, red pepper slices, mozzarella and cheddar onto the pizza bases. Finally, top with chilli.
● At The Watch House, we slide the pizzas into our wood oven for around 45 seconds before turning and firing them for another 45 seconds. But, in a conventional oven, you'll need to leave it in for 15 minutes or so – until the base is crispy and the cheese on top has melted.
● Remove the pizzas and place them on boards, then top each with rocket before serving.

PULLED PORK PIZZA

MAKES 2 PIZZAS

There's not much to say about this fabulous pizza. Its flavour speaks for itself…

INGREDIENTS

1 pork shoulder joint, deboned
1 clove garlic, crushed
1 tbsp smoked paprika
400g tinned chopped tomatoes
2 onions, finely chopped
2 apples, peeled, cored and quartered
4 tbsp cider vinegar
1 tsp white mustard seeds
1 tsp cumin seeds

1 sprig thyme, chopped
2 bay leaves
Brown sugar
Worcester sauce
Pizza dough (see page 17)
½ red onion, thinly sliced
Small tin sweetcorn, drained
140g mozzarella, sliced
60g cheddar, grated

● Preheat your oven to 160°C/320°F.
● Score the fat on the pork and place it in a roasting tin with high sides. Rub the pork with the garlic, paprika, sea salt and black pepper, and surround it with the tomatoes, onions, apples, cider vinegar, mustard and cumin seeds, thyme and bay leaves. Add a sprinkle of brown sugar and a dash of Worcester sauce. Cover the roasting tin with foil and crimp tightly around the edges. Repeat with another layer of foil. Put the pork in the oven for at least 5 hours.
● Remove the pork from the oven and remove from the roasting tin to cool. Retain the cooking liquid and set aside in the fridge. Shred the pork using a fork or your fingers. Set aside.
● Turn your oven up to 200°C/400°F. If you're using a wood oven, bring it up to 400°C/800°F.
● Once the cooking liquid has cooled, remove any fat from the top and pour it into a saucepan. Bring to the boil, stirring to avoid burning, then add more sugar and reduce until it reaches a thick consistency.
● Roll the pizza dough out onto a cold surface sprinkled with semolina to prevent it from sticking. Create two pizza bases by rolling the dough out as thinly as possible.
● Spread the barbecue sauce onto the pizza bases, and top each with around 100g pulled pork, the red onions and sweetcorn. Finish with the mozzarella and cheddar.
● At The Watch House, we slide the pizzas into our wood oven for around 45 seconds before turning and firing them for another 45 seconds. But, in a conventional oven, you'll need to leave it in for 15 minutes or so – until the base is crispy and the cheese on top has melted.
● Remove the pizzas and place them on boards. Serve immediately.

ROASTED BUTTERNUT SQUASH, COURGETTE & FETA PIZZA

SERVES 4

This pizza may be meat-free, but you don't have to be a vegetarian to enjoy its stunning combination of flavours. Go easy on the chilli if you're serving it to younger children.

INGREDIENTS

¼ butternut squash, cut into small cubes
Olive oil
Pizza dough (see page 17)
Tomato sauce (see page 17)
8 cherry tomatoes, cut in half
100g feta, cut into cubes

1 courgette
70g mozzarella, sliced
30g cheddar, grated
1 chilli, finely sliced
1 sprig thyme, finely chopped
1 sprig mint, finely chopped

- Preheat your oven to 180°C/350°F.
- Arrange the butternut squash cubes on a roasting tray and drizzle with olive oil. Roast in the oven for around 25 minutes until tender. Set aside.
- Turn the oven up to 200°C/400°F. If you're using a wood oven, bring it up to 400°C/800°F.
- Roll the pizza dough out onto a cold surface sprinkled with semolina to prevent it from sticking. Create two pizza bases by rolling the dough out as thinly as possible (this ensures crispiness).
- Spread tomato sauce onto the pizza bases, then arrange the butternut squash cubes, cherry tomatoes and feta on top.
- To make the courgette ribbons, take a potato peeler and peel thin ribbons of courgette straight onto the pizza. Top with the mozzarella and cheddar.
- Sprinkle on the chilli, thyme and mint. All work wonderfully with the other flavours in the pizza, so don't hold back.
- At The Watch House, we slide the pizzas into our wood oven for around 45 seconds before turning and firing them for another 45 seconds. But, in a conventional oven, you'll need to leave it in for 15 minutes or so – until the base is crispy and the cheese on top has melted.
- Remove the pizzas and place them on boards. Serve immediately.

THE PISCES PIZZA

MAKES 2 PIZZAS

As its name suggests, this pizza is all about the fish and seafood that's found in the waters just a few feet from The Hive and The Watch House. Feel free to experiment with different shellfish in this dish – so long as they're fresh, they'll taste amazing.

INGREDIENTS

2 large handfuls mussels
Glass white wine
1 clove garlic, crushed
200g butter
2 small squid (see page 12)
Pizza dough (see page 17)

Tomato sauce (see page 17)
8–10 cooked king prawns, peeled
140g mozzarella, sliced
60g cheddar, grated
Small bunch parsley, chopped
2 lemons, cut into wedges

● Wash the mussels in cold water and discard any that do not close when tapped.

● Preheat your oven to 200°C/400°F. If you're using a wood oven, bring it up to 400°C/800°F.

● Preheat a large saucepan and pour in the white wine. Add the mussels. Cover and cook for 2–3 minutes, until the mussels have opened. Remove from the heat and discard any that remain closed.

● Extract the mussels from their shells. Retain the meat and set aside in a warm place.

● Combine the garlic with the butter. Set aside.

● Cut the squid into thin rings. Preheat a sauté pan until it's smoking-hot.

● Melt the garlic butter in the pan then add the squid rings. Fry for 1 minute.

● Roll the pizza dough out onto a cold surface sprinkled with semolina to prevent it from sticking. Create two pizza bases by rolling the dough out as thinly as possible (this ensures crispiness).

● Spread tomato sauce onto the pizza bases, then arrange the king prawns, squid rings, mussels, mozzarella and cheddar on top.

● At The Watch House, we slide the pizzas into our wood oven for around 45 seconds before turning and firing them for another 45 seconds. But, in a conventional oven, you'll need to leave it in for 15 minutes or so – until the base is crispy and the cheese on top has melted.

● Remove the pizzas and place them on boards, then sprinkle each with the parsley. Serve immediately with lemon wedges on the side.

THE SIESTA PIZZA

MAKES 2 PIZZAS

You're likely to want a siesta after eating this delicious, Mediterranean-inspired pizza; its wonderfully herby flavours evoke those lazy, hazy, summer days in Southern Europe. Something of an antipasti board in pizza form, it undoubtedly benefits from an investment in superior ingredients. At The Watch House we use Tomorroso cherry tomatoes as we believe the taste far outweighs the cost; and we've found that you get what you pay for when it comes to Parma ham. As we always make this pizza in a wood oven, we've found it tends to puff up like a balloon during cooking – so we've had to become experts in deflating it with a well-aimed jab of a log hook.

INGREDIENTS

200ml olive oil
6 cloves garlic, peeled
Good handful fresh parsley, chopped
3 sprigs rosemary
3-4 sprigs thyme
Pizza dough (see page 17)

4 pieces Parma ham
20 black olives, pitted
20 sun-dried tomatoes
100g feta, cubed
100g rocket, washed
Your favourite salad dressing

● Preheat your oven to 200°C/400°F. If you're using a wood oven, bring it up to 400°C/800°F.
● To make the garlic-and-herb oil, add the olive oil, garlic, parsley, and rosemary and thyme to a large bowl, then whiz with a small hand blender until you have a smooth green paste with no large lumps.
● Roll the pizza dough out onto a cold surface sprinkled with semolina to prevent it from sticking. Create two pizza bases by rolling the dough out as thinly as possible (this ensures crispiness).
● Spread the garlic-and-herb oil onto the pizza bases. Don't be too generous, though, or the oil will end up on the base of your oven. Add a small sprinkle of sea salt.
● At The Watch House, we slide the pizzas into our wood oven for around 45 seconds before turning and firing them for another 45 seconds. But, in a conventional oven, you'll need to leave it in for 15 minutes or so – until the base is crispy and golden.
● Remove the pizzas and place them on boards, then top each with ripped pieces of Parma ham, olives, sun-dried tomatoes, feta and rocket. Add a splash of your favourite salad dressing and serve immediately.

HAM & PINEAPPLE PIZZA WITH A TWIST

MAKES 2 PIZZAS

As guilty a pleasure as listening to a Barry Manilow CD in the bath with a glass of Babycham, the ham and pineapple pizza has never been a stylish dish. That doesn't mean it isn't incredibly tasty, though. And if you use good-quality ingredients such as thickly sliced farmhouse ham and fresh pineapple, you can take it to a whole new level. The twist we've added here is a big dollop of fiery homemade guacamole, which not only looks fantastic, but also works wonderfully with the saltiness of the ham and the sharpness of the pineapple. Enjoy a slice with a glass of cold cider.

INGREDIENTS

Pizza dough (see page 17)
Tomato sauce (see page 17)
2 slices good-quality ham, ripped into small pieces
½ fresh pineapple, trimmed and cubed
70g mozzarella, sliced

30g cheddar, grated
1 ripe avocado, diced
1 red chilli, finely diced
1 small red onion, finely diced
Small handful coriander, roughly chopped
1 lime, juiced

● Preheat your oven to 200°C/400°F. If you're using a wood oven, bring it up to 400°C/800°F.
● Roll the pizza dough out onto a cold surface sprinkled with semolina to prevent it from sticking. Create two pizza bases by rolling the dough out as thinly as possible (this ensures crispiness).
● Spread the tomato sauce, ham, fresh pineapple cubes, mozzarella and cheddar onto the pizza bases.
● To make the guacamole, roughly combine the avocado, chilli, red onion, coriander and lime juice in a bowl. Season to taste.
● At The Watch House, we slide the pizzas into our wood oven for around 45 seconds before turning and firing them for another 45 seconds. But, in a conventional oven, you'll need to leave it in for 15 minutes or so – until the base is crispy and the cheese on top has melted.
● Remove the pizzas and place them on boards, then add a big spoonful of guacamole to the middle of each before serving.

CHARGRILLED STEAK & BALSAMIC RED ONION PIZZA

MAKES 2 PIZZAS

There's no substitute for steak when you're hungry – so it's no surprise this pizza, topped with sirloin strips, flies out of the kitchen whenever we chalk it up on the menu.

INGREDIENTS

1 sirloin steak

2 red onions, finely sliced

1 clove garlic, peeled and crushed

100ml balsamic vinegar

2 tbsp caster sugar

50–75ml crème fraîche

1 tsp horseradish sauce

Pizza dough (see page 17)

Tomato sauce (see page 17)

2 cooked field mushrooms, sliced

4 cherry tomatoes, quartered

70g mozzarella, sliced

30g cheddar, grated

Small bunch watercress, washed

● Preheat your oven to 200°C/400°F. If you're using a wood oven, bring it up to 400°C/800°F.
● Heat a chargrill or griddle pan until smoking hot. Season the steak on both sides and place on the chargrill for 1 minute, then turn and cook for another minute. Remove and leave to cool. Once cooled, cut the steak into thin slices.
● Sweat the onions and garlic in a drop of olive oil for about 5 minutes, until soft. Then add the balsamic vinegar and sugar, and keep on the heat until most of the liquid has reduced and it starts to resemble a sticky chutney. Remove from the heat and leave to cool.
● Mix the crème fraîche and horseradish sauce together.
● Roll the dough out onto a cold surface sprinkled with semolina to prevent it from sticking. Create two pizza bases by rolling the dough out as thinly as possible (this ensures crispiness).
● Spread tomato sauce onto the pizza bases, then arrange the steak slices, field mushrooms, cherry tomatoes, balsamic red onions, mozzarella and cheddar on top.
● At The Watch House, we slide the pizzas into our wood oven for around 45 seconds before turning and firing them for another 45 seconds. But, in a conventional oven, you'll need to leave it in for 15 minutes or so – until the base is crispy and the cheese on top has melted.
● Remove the pizzas and place them on boards, then top each with a good handful of watercress and a few small spoonfuls of the horseradish crème fraîche.

SMOKED HADDOCK & POTATO PIZZA

MAKES 2 PIZZAS

Sturdy and salty, this is one of the biggest sellers at The Watch House on days when there's a chill in the air. Add some crispy smoked bacon or lardons for an extra boost of flavour.

INGREDIENTS

1 fillet smoked haddock, skinned
600ml milk
1 bay leaf
2 large potatoes, peeled and cut into
2cm cubes
1 leek, finely sliced
Olive oil
100ml crème fraîche

Wholegrain mustard
Pizza dough (see page 17)
1 small tin sweetcorn, drained
140g mozzarella, sliced
60g cheddar, grated
Small bunch chives, chopped
1 lemon, cut into wedges

● Preheat your oven to 200°C/400°F. If you're using a wood oven, bring it up to 400°C/800°F.
● Place the haddock into a pan with the milk and bay leaf, and gently bring up to the boil. Around 1 minute after the liquid reaches boiling point, remove the fish with a slotted spoon, flake and set aside in a warm place.
● Put the potato cubes into the milk and cook until tender. Remove and discard the liquid.
● In a sauté pan, sweat the leek with a drop of olive oil until soft. Set aside.
● Combine the crème fraîche with 1 tsp wholegrain mustard and set aside.
● Roll the pizza dough out onto a cold surface sprinkled with semolina to prevent it from sticking. Create two pizza bases by rolling the dough out as thinly as possible.
● Spread a thin layer of the mustard crème fraîche onto the pizza bases and sprinkle the potato cubes liberally on top. Arrange the smoked haddock flakes, leeks and sweetcorn over this and add the mozzarella and cheddar. Finish with a sprinkle of chives.
● At The Watch House, we slide the pizzas into our wood oven for around 45 seconds before turning and firing them for another 45 seconds. But, in a conventional oven, you'll need to leave it in for 15 minutes or so – until the base is crispy and the cheese on top has melted.
● Remove the pizzas and place them on boards. Serve with lemon wedges on the side.

THE MAVERICK PIZZA

MAKES 2 PIZZAS

It might sound like an odd mix, but the flavours of beetroot, smoked mackerel, feta and horseradish crème fraîche in The Watch House's famous Maverick Pizza really do go well together. It helps that the mackerel we use comes from the Chesil Smokery in just-down-the-road Bridport – where the distinctive taste of the fish and the delicious texture of its flesh is brought out by days of smoking over oak chips – and we suggest you source something equally wonderful for your creation. But even if you were to use the vacuum-packed stuff from your local supermarket, this pizza would still taste great.

INGREDIENTS

2 cooked beetroots, peeled
Horseradish sauce
100ml crème fraîche
Small bunch chives, finely chopped
Pizza dough (see page 17)
1–2 smoked mackerel fillets, skinned and flaked

100g feta, cubed
70g mozzarella, sliced
30g cheddar, grated
Small bunch watercress, washed
1 lemon, cut into wedges

● Preheat your oven to 200°C/400°F. If you're using a wood oven, bring it up to 400°C/800°F.
● Make the beetroot sauce by roughly chopping the cooked beetroot and placing it in a blender. Add a sprinkle of sea salt, a good twist of pepper, 1 tsp horseradish sauce and just cover with water. Blend until you have a smooth purée, then season to taste. If the purée is too thick, simply add a little more water.
● Mix the crème fraîche with horseradish sauce to get the kick you prefer, then add the chives.
● Roll the pizza dough out onto a cold surface sprinkled with semolina to prevent it from sticking. Create two pizza bases by rolling the dough out as thinly as possible (this ensures crispiness).
● Spread the beetroot sauce, smoked mackerel flakes and feta onto the pizza bases, and top with mozzarella and cheddar.
● At The Watch House, we slide the pizzas into our wood oven for around 45 seconds before turning and firing them for another 45 seconds. But, in a conventional oven, you'll need to leave it in for 15 minutes or so – until the base is crispy and the cheese on top has melted.
● Remove the pizzas and place them on boards, then top each with a good handful of watercress, a few small spoonfuls of the horseradish crème fraîche and a lemon wedge.

WILD MUSHROOM, SPINACH & SOFT POACHED EGG PIZZA

SERVES 4

This wonderful creation showcases the earthy flavours of the wild mushrooms that grow plentifully in West Dorset throughout the year. Don't be tempted to pick them from woods, though, unless you've got a mushrooming expert with you. We're all for foraged ingredients at The Hive, but eating the wrong kind of fungi can be dangerous. Get your mushrooms instead from local markets or farm shops, where the taste – and your good health – can be assured.

INGREDIENTS

White wine vinegar

Butter

3–4 handfuls wild mushrooms

2 eggs

Pizza dough (see page 17)

Tomato sauce (see page 17)

100g spinach, washed

140g mozzarella, sliced

60g cheddar, grated

● Preheat your oven to 200°C/400°F. If you're using a wood oven, bring it up to 400°C/800°F.
● Bring a pan of water to the boil and add a splash of white wine vinegar.
● Melt a knob of butter in a smoking-hot frying pan and sauté the wild mushrooms. Season to taste and set aside.
● Carefully crack the eggs into the pan of boiling water and poach for 2–3 minutes. Remove from the pan and place them into ice-cold water to stop them cooking any further. Leave for at least 5 minutes then place the eggs on a tea towel to dry.
● Roll the pizza dough out onto a cold surface sprinkled with semolina to prevent it from sticking. Create two pizza bases by rolling the dough out as thinly as possible.
● Spread tomato sauce onto the pizza bases then arrange the spinach, wild mushrooms, mozzarella and cheddar on top. Finish each pizza with an egg.
● At The Watch House, we slide pizzas into our wood oven for around 45 seconds before turning and firing them for another 45. But, in a conventional oven, you'll need to leave it in for 15 minutes or so – until the base is crispy and the eggs are warm but have a runny yolk.
● Remove the pizzas and place them on boards. Serve immediately.

CROWD-PLEASERS

HOT & COLD SEAFOOD PLATTER

SERVES 4

It doesn't matter what time of year it is; there will always be someone at The Hive or The Watch House tucking into one of our legendary seafood platters. We shared the secrets of the individual hot and cold versions in our first cookbook, but this combination of the two is equally popular. Our customers may love the clean, fresh taste of Dorset lobster, Weymouth crab and River Yealm oysters – especially with a bowl of creamy mayonnaise and a glass of cold, crisp white wine on the side – but they adore piping-hot Lyme Bay scallops, too. Who can blame them?

INGREDIENTS

Mayonnaise (see page 15)
2 whole lobsters
2 whole crabs
8 oysters
250g samphire
8 scallops

Olive oil
Butter
2 lemons, cut into wedges
12 crevette prawns
8 langoustines

- Prepare your mayonnaise according to the instructions on page 15. Set aside.
- Prepare the lobster, crabs and oysters according to the instructions on pages 12, 13 and 14 or, alternatively, ask your fishmonger to do it for you.
- Take a large dish or wooden board and arrange the samphire on top. At The Hive, we like to use this vibrant, green edible plant as a base for our platters as it provides a wonderful splash of coastal colour.
- Preheat a large, heavy-bottomed frying pan over a high heat. Season the scallops with sea salt and olive oil, and place them into the hot frying pan. Turn each scallop after 45–60 seconds (depending on their size). Make sure the scallops are golden-brown where they've been in contact with pan, and have an even colour on both sides.
- Add a knob of butter and squeeze of lemon after another 45-60 seconds, then remove from the heat and leave to stand for 30 seconds.
- Have fun arranging the lobster, crab, oysters, crevette prawns and langoustines on top of the samphire, then add the hot scallops. When you're happy with your creation, serve it up immediately with crusty bread, lemon wedges and a big bowl of mayonnaise.

CRISPY SALMON WITH WATERCRESS CRÈME FRAÎCHE

SERVES 4

The key to this tasty dish is to get the salmon skin as crispy as possible. The additional punch of flavour this delivers alongside that of the delicate, pink flesh of the fish is well worth a bit of extra effort when you start preparing. Children – even little ones – absolutely love this dish, and you could even get them involved in making the crème fraîche with you. The scoring of the fish is most definitely an adult job, though; as is checking the fillets for any stray bones before serving it up to the family.

INGREDIENTS

4 salmon fillets, scaled and pin-boned
2 bunches watercress
100g crème fraîche

1 lemon, juiced
Olive oil

● Preheat a non-stick frying pan. To get the salmon fillets nice and crispy, you will need to score the skin. With the skin-side up, roll the fillet slightly and make a cut around half an inch deep with a sharp knife. Don't cut completely across the skin. Score the skin several times in this way.
● To make the watercress crème fraîche, remove the stalks from 1 bunch of watercress and place in a bowl with the crème fraîche. Blitz with a hand-held blender, then add half the lemon juice and a pinch of cracked black pepper. Season to taste then set aside in the fridge.
● Oil and season the salmon fillets, and arrange them skin-side down in the hot pan. Don't turn until they're cooked two-thirds through (when the flesh is beginning to change from a translucent colour to a more solid one). Then turn down the heat and let them cook through slowly.
● Place the salmon fillets onto a board, garnish with the leftover watercress and squeeze over the rest of the lemon juice. Serve with a pot of the watercress crème fraîche.

SHRIMP BURGERS WITH LEMON MAYONNAISE

SERVES 4

It's the extra bite provided by the ginger and chillies in this recipe that makes our shrimp burgers special. A bestseller at the café, they are ordered on warm summer days when people want something light to accompany their cold glass of wine out on the terrace. But they're just as popular on cold winter afternoons when their subtle spiciness comes into its own.

INGREDIENTS

600g shrimps or prawns
3 cloves garlic
2 medium onions, diced
2 red chillies, finely chopped
3cm piece root ginger, grated

4 lemons, juiced
Mayonnaise (see page 15)
Olive oil
4–6 handfuls mixed salad leaves
4 burger buns, sliced

● Place the shrimps in a colander and rinse, then pick up a handful at a time and squeeze hard to get rid of as much water as possible.

● Put the shrimps into a food processor and blitz. Pour into a mixing bowl.

● Crush the garlic cloves and blend with a pinch of sea salt, then add to the shrimp mixture. Mix in the onions, chillies, ginger and the juice of 2 lemons, then set aside in the fridge.

● Prepare your mayonnaise according to the instructions on page 15, then combine 4 tbsp of it with the juice of 2 lemons. Adjust to taste.

● Preheat a large frying pan over a high heat. Take the shrimp mixture from the fridge and shape into 4 burger patties.

● Drizzle a little olive oil into the pan and put in the shrimp burgers. Fry until the sides in contact with the pan turn a golden-brown colour, then flip over and cook for another 4–5 minutes. Cut into one of the burgers to check they have cooked through.

● Arrange the salad leaves in the burger buns and add a generous helping of lemon mayonnaise. Place the shrimp burgers into the buns and serve with lemon wedges.

KING PRAWN &
MONKFISH SKEWERS

SERVES 4

This dish is a real treat – and the cooking process is absolutely perfect for children to get involved in. Threading the juicy king prawns and the tender chunks of monkfish onto the skewers is a lot of fun and you can either follow The Hive method (two monkfish pieces sandwiched between three king prawns) or create your own design – perhaps including cherry tomatoes or pancetta. This recipe requires 8 skewers, but if you're using the wooden variety, soak them in water for at least an hour before you start preparing this dish. This will prevent them from burning.

INGREDIENTS

24 king prawns, peeled

16 chunks monkfish tail

2 red chillies, deseeded and finely chopped

3 limes, zested and juiced

Olive oil

1 bunch coriander, chopped

100g samphire

● Thread the king prawns and monkfish onto the skewers. Set aside on a baking tray.

● Next make the marinade. Put the chillies, lime zest and juice, and a drizzle of olive oil into a bowl. Add half the coriander, then season with sea salt and freshly ground black pepper. Mix well and pour over the skewers.

● Preheat a frying pan over a high heat. Place the skewers into the pan and fry till golden-brown on each side. Check the king prawns and monkfish are cooked. They should feel firm when you press them. Remove from the pan and set aside on a large serving dish.

● Flash-fry the samphire for a couple of minutes in the same frying pan, then arrange on a large serving dish.

● Place the skewers on top and scatter with the rest of the coriander. Serve immediately.

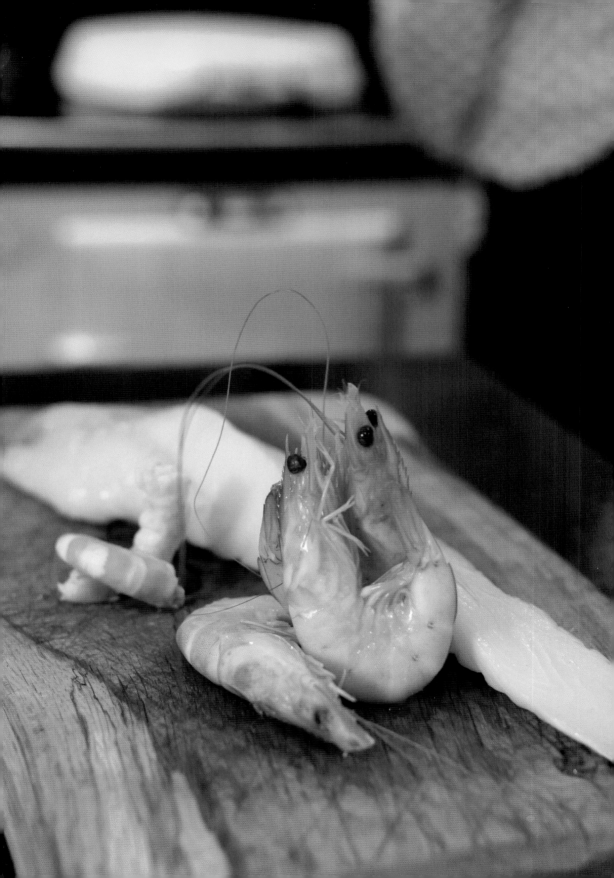

PAELLA

SERVES 4

Yes, we know this is a traditional Spanish dish, created from the meat, seafood and rice found in abundance in the port city of Valencia. But we have excellent shellfish, chicken and pork in Dorset, too – and we've found this dish is the perfect showcase for them. Leave out the mussels and squid if your kids are squeamish about their slightly rubbery texture.

INGREDIENTS

500g mussels

6 boneless chicken breasts or thighs, skin on and quartered

Plain flour, for dusting

Olive oil

100g chorizo, sliced

6 slices pancetta

1 onion, finely chopped

4 cloves garlic, finely chopped

2 large pinches saffron

2l hot chicken stock

1 heaped tsp smoked paprika

500g paella rice

2 handfuls fresh or frozen peas

10 king prawns

2 small squid, halved and scored

1 small bunch flat-leaf parsley, chopped

2 lemons, cut into wedges

● Wash the mussels in cold water and discard any that do not close when tapped.

● Preheat your oven to 190°C/375°F. Season the chicken pieces and dust with flour.

● Heat a little olive oil in a large, deep pan and fry the chicken until golden-brown on both sides. Remove the pieces from the pan and arrange on a baking tray. Bake in the oven for 30 minutes.

● Return the pan to the heat. Add the chorizo and pancetta, and fry until browned and crispy. Put in the onion and garlic, and cook until soft.

● Mix half the saffron with the hot chicken stock.

● Pour the saffron-infused chicken stock into the pan with the chorizo and pancetta, then add the smoked paprika and rice, and leave to cook over a medium heat. Stir occasionally.

● After around 20 minutes, when the rice has nearly cooked, pour in the rest of the stock along with the peas, king prawns, mussels and squid. Cover and cook for 10 minutes more.

● Add the cooked chicken and serve immediately sprinkled with chopped flat-leaf parsley and with lemon wedges on the side.

LARGE FISH PIE

SERVES 6

You'll need a big dish for this mammoth fish pie – one that will comfortably hold enough for six people – so make sure you've got one large enough. If not, you might have to borrow one. Any inconvenience, though, is more than worth it. Nothing can beat the taste of firm-textured salmon and cod blended with juicy prawns and herbs, and topped with steaming-hot cheesy mashed potato.

INGREDIENTS

500g salmon, scaled, pin-boned and diced
500g cod, scaled, pin-boned and diced
250g prawns, washed and peeled
250g smoked salmon
1 heaped tbsp chives, chopped
1 heaped tbsp tarragon, chopped
1 large onion, diced

1 bunch spring onions, chopped
1 clove garlic, finely chopped
1 large glass white wine
400ml double cream
400ml crème fraîche
1kg potatoes, peeled
75g strong cheddar, grated

● Ensure the salmon and cod are properly diced. You can ask you fishmonger to do this for you. Preheat your oven to 180°C/350°F.

● In a large mixing bowl, combine the salmon, cod, prawns and smoked salmon with the herbs, onion, spring onions and garlic. Mix well and season with sea salt and freshly ground black pepper. Arrange this mixture evenly at the base of the pie dish.

● Pour the white wine into a saucepan over a medium heat and reduce by half. Add the cream, 300ml crème fraîche, more salt and pepper, and whisk together to avoid the sauce splitting. Continue cooking for another 4 minutes until it starts to thicken.

● Pour the creamy sauce over the raw fish mixture. Mix together and set aside in the fridge for 30 minutes.

● Boil the potatoes until soft then drain. Mash until light and fluffy, then add the remaining crème fraîche. Mix well and season to taste.

● Spread the mashed potato over the top of the fish and cream sauce mixture, sprinkle with the grated cheese and bake in the oven for 20–25 minutes until the pie is golden-brown and piping-hot throughout.

● Serve the pie in its dish with lots of steamed green vegetables.

THE HIVE
OYSTER BOARD

SERVES 4

Our position on England's southwest coast means we are ideally placed for some of the finest – and tastiest – native oysters in the country. We get our bivalves from nearby Lyme Bay and Devon's River Yealm, and serve them up to customers in a huge variety of ways. By far the most popular, though, is the couldn't-be-simpler-to-prepare platter of freshly shucked oysters with a couple of tart dressings on the side. So that's what we've recreated here. The accompanying tequila shooters are for adults only, obviously.

INGREDIENTS

Seaweed, washed
2 shallots, diced
100ml red wine vinegar
Tequila
2 limes, juiced

Caster sugar
24 oysters
Crushed ice, for display
2 lemons, cut into wedges

● Bring a large saucepan of salted water up to the boil. Add the seaweed and bring it back to the boil. Strain and drop the seaweed into cold water to refresh it. Set aside in a cold place.
● To make the dressing, add the shallots to the red wine vinegar and mix. Pour into a ramekin.
● To make the accompanying shooters, combine the tequila, lime juice and 1 tsp sugar in shot glasses and mix until all the sugar has dissolved.
● Shuck the oysters according to the instructions on page 14.
● Drain the seaweed. Arrange the crushed ice onto a large platter, cover with the seaweed and place the shucked oysters on top.
● Serve immediately with the dressing and tequila shooters. And don't forget lemon wedges and a bottle of Tabasco sauce, too.

TWO CANAPÉS

SERVES 4

ROASTED RED PEPPER SHOTS

Ingredients

1 onion, roughly chopped

1 tbsp olive oil

3 cloves garlic, crushed

1 tbsp sugar

2 tbsp red pepper pesto

400g can plum tomatoes

295g jar roasted red peppers, drained
and chopped

200ml vegetable stock

● Fry the onion in the olive oil for 8–10 minutes, then add the garlic, sugar and red pepper pesto to the pan, and cook for 1–2 minutes. Pour in the plum tomatoes, roasted red peppers and vegetable stock and simmer for 10 minutes. Season.

● Blitz with a hand-held blender until smooth, then set aside to cool. Freeze in freezer bags or a microwaveable container.

● Defrost before serving, then reheat gently in a pan, stirring frequently, until piping-hot. Serve in shot glasses or miniature beakers.

TERIYAKI BEEF & LETTUCE PARCELS

Ingredients

350g sirloin steak, trimmed

2 tbsp teriyaki sauce marinade

½ cucumber

2 tbsp coriander, roughly chopped

½ lime, juiced

6 Little Gem lettuce leaves

1 red chilli, deseeded and thinly sliced

½ red onion, thinly sliced

● Put the steak between two sheets of clingfilm and beat with a rolling pin until it's half its original thickness. Thinly slice it, then mix with the teriyaki marinade in a bowl. Leave it to marinate for 5–10 minutes.

● Roughly chop the cucumber and mix with the coriander and lime juice. Season with sea salt.

● Heat a frying pan until very hot, then fry the steak slices for 1½–2½ minutes (rare to medium), turning the slices halfway through.

● Pile the cucumber mixture into the lettuce leaves, then top with the seared teriyaki beef, chilli and red onion.

TWO MORE CANAPÉS

SERVES 4

CRAB SALSA CROSTINI

Ingredients

250g pot fresh crabmeat

85g cherry tomatoes, quartered

1 small red onion, finely chopped

4 thin baguettes

Olive oil

1 lime, zested and juiced

Bunch coriander, chopped

● Combine the crabmeat, tomatoes and red onion and set aside in the fridge for up to 2 days.

● To make the crostini bases, cut each of the baguettes into 20 ½cm-thick slices. Drizzle with olive oil and place under the grill for 2–3 minutes until golden, then turn them over and grill for another 1–2 minutes.

● When you're ready to serve, mix the lime zest and juice, and chopped coriander into the crabmeat mixture, then pile onto the crostini.

PARMA HAM & PARMESAN PALMIERS

Ingredients

1 packet ready-to-roll puff pastry

Dijon mustard

2 tbsp Parmesan cheese, grated

6 slices Parma ham

1 egg, beaten with a pinch of salt

● Preheat your oven to 200°C/400°F.

● Roll the pastry out flat and spread each half with a little mustard. Sprinkle generously with Parmesan and lay a slice of Parma ham on top.

● Roll the pastry up tightly so that it resembles a sausage. Wrap in clingfilm and set aside in the fridge for 15 minutes to chill.

● Using a sharp knife, cut into 2cm-thick slices. Arrange the slices on a baking tray and brush with the beaten egg. Bake for 10 minutes until golden-brown and crispy. Sprinkle with a little Parmesan and serve.

FISH DOGS

MAKES 4 HOT DOGS

This fishy take on the traditional hot dog has proved extremely popular both at The Hive and The Watch House, and whenever we serve it from our Silver Dreams vintage Airstream trailer at outdoor events. People have queued for the best part of an hour just to get their hands on one of these piping-hot snacks, wrapped in a serviette and oozing with our homemade tartare sauce, just because they've seen others eating them. We use hake because it's relatively inexpensive and sustainable, but this dish could be made with any good-quality, firm white fish.

INGREDIENTS

Tartare sauce (see page 16)
Sunflower oil, for deep-frying
Handful plain flour
2 hake fillets, cut in half lengthways

Breadcrumbs
3 eggs
4 hot dog rolls, sliced open
1 cos lettuce, chopped

● Prepare your tartare sauce according to the instructions on page 16. Set aside in the fridge until you're ready to use it.
● Preheat the sunflower oil to 180°C/350°F in a large pan or deep-fat fryer.
● Put the plain flour onto a plate and season with sea salt and freshly ground black pepper. Roll the hake fillets in the flour and shake off any excess.
● Get a plate of breadcrumbs ready. Whisk the eggs together in a shallow bowl. Roll the hake fillets in the eggs then the breadcrumbs. Ensure they're completely covered.
● Place the hake fillets into the pan or deep-fat fryer and cook for around 4–5 minutes, until golden-brown and crisp.
● Put a hake piece in each hot dog roll, then add the chopped lettuce and plenty of homemade tartare sauce. Serve immediately.

KING PRAWN CURRY

SERVES 4

One for families with older children who relish a spicy supper, this delicious and warming curry brings out the flavour of juicy king prawns in the most stunning way. Serve it with plenty of white rice, and some poppadoms and naan bread on the side. And don't forget some ice-cold beers for the grown-ups, too.

INGREDIENTS

600g raw king prawns, peeled
6 tbsp yoghurt
4–5 green chillies, finely sliced
4 tbsp olive or sunflower oil
½ tsp cumin seeds
2 medium onions, finely chopped

2–3 large cloves garlic, crushed
1 tsp turmeric
2 tsp garam masala
2 medium tomatoes, roughly chopped
½ tsp dried chilli flakes
Small bunch coriander, finely chopped

● First marinade the king prawns. Rinse and drain the prawns, then pat them dry and place them in a bowl. Add the yoghurt, 2 chillies and ½ teaspoon of salt. Mix well, cover and leave overnight in the fridge.
● Pour the olive or sunflower oil into a heavy-based pan (around 25cm in diameter) and warm over a medium heat.
● Spoon in the cumin seeds then swirl and brown for 10 seconds. Add the onions and sauté for about 10 minutes until browned all over.
● Add the garlic, reduce the heat to low and stir. Fry for 2 minutes. Mix in the turmeric and cook for 1 minute.
● Add the remaining green chillies, then increase the heat to medium and cook for 1 minute. Mix in 1½ tsp garam masala and cook for a further minute.
● Put in ¼ tsp salt, the tomatoes and chilli flakes, and cook for 2 minutes. Pour in 120ml boiling water and mix well.
● Bring the sauce up to a gentle simmer and leave for 3 minutes, then add another ¼ tsp salt. Stir in the marinated king prawns and the rest of the yoghurt marinade, and cook over a medium heat until the prawns are opaque and have cooked through.
● Sprinkle over the remaining garam masala and stir. Fold in the coriander and serve immediately with fluffy white rice.

CAKES &
PUDDINGS

CHOCOLATE & CHERRY TIFFIN

SERVES 8–10

You don't even have to turn on the oven to make this easy-peasy, no-bake dish. Tiffin – otherwise known as chocolate refrigerator cake – is a super-indulgent treat and it's ideal to make with the kids. All you need is a spare half hour, your favourite fillings (we love the combination of chocolate and cherry), and space in the fridge to chill. Feel free to mix and match fillings according to your taste – try adding stem ginger, apricots, pistachios, pecans or even crushed Maltesers. Be warned, though; this cake manages to be both very rich and extremely moreish.

INGREDIENTS

25g butter
250g dark chocolate
400g digestive biscuits, broken into small pieces

110g golden syrup
110g glacé cherries, chopped
200g sultanas
300g milk chocolate

● Line a 33cm baking tin with greaseproof paper.
● Bring a saucepan of water up to a gentle simmer. Place the butter and dark chocolate into a heatproof bowl, and put this on top of the saucepan to create a bain marie. Melt the chocolate and butter, stirring occasionally. Remove from the heat and set aside for a couple of minutes to cool.
● Add the digestive biscuits, syrup, cherries and sultanas to the chocolate mixture and mix well. Spoon the chocolate mixture into the baking tin and level with the back of the spoon.
● Cover the mixture with a piece of greaseproof paper and, using either a rolling pin or your hands, press down until it fits snugly into the tin and the top is as flat as possible. Put it into the fridge for at least 4 hours to chill.
● When the tiffin has set and is firm to the touch, bring another saucepan of water up to a gentle simmer. Put the milk chocolate into a heatproof bowl, and place this on top of the saucepan to create a bain marie. Once melted, pour it over the tiffin and use a spoon to spread it evenly. Chill in the fridge for a further 15 minutes.
● Cut the tiffin into individual slices with a warm knife. It is now ready to serve.

BAKED ALASKA

SERVES 8–10

This pudding of ice cream topped with meringue is a real show-stopper. At The Watch House, we bake it in our wood-fired pizza oven where, to the delight of anyone watching, it cooks and puffs up in a matter of seconds. And its delicious sweet scent is enough to make everyone reach for the dessert menu. You can serve it with fresh fruit, thick cream or – as we do at the café – totally unadorned. And, though we're assuming you don't have a pizza oven to fire it in at home, you will need a crème brûlée-style blowtorch to flame the meringue and give it that wonderfully scorched look.

INGREDIENTS

4 egg whites
115g white sugar
115g soft brown sugar

1 large sponge base
Your favourite ice cream

● Have your blowtorch to hand. Or, if you're lucky enough to be using a wood oven, bring it up to 400°C/800°F.
● Bring a saucepan of water up to a gentle simmer. Put the egg whites and sugar into a heatproof bowl, and put this on top of the saucepan to create a bain marie. Dissolve the sugar, stirring occasionally, but don't allow the mixture to come to a boil.
● Remove from the heat and, with an electric whisk, whisk for 6–8 minutes until thick and glossy, and the mixture starts forming stiff peaks.
● Place your sponge base onto a baking tray and pile a mountain of ice cream on top.
● Pipe or spoon the meringue all over the ice cream to cover it. Take the blowtorch and flame the meringue all over until it turns a golden-brown colour. Alternatively, put it into the wood oven to achieve the same effect.
● Serve immediately with lots of fanfare.

GINGERBREAD MEN

SERVES 8–10

It's unlikely you'll find another recipe in this book more child-friendly than this one. Our famous gingerbread men are loved by The Hive's junior diners and have prevented many a lunchtime meltdown from those who aren't as used to waiting for food as their parents – and they're equally popular as a takeaway item, too. The smell of freshly baked gingerbread when we take the 'men' out of the oven is the best possible advert for this dish. It only takes the merest scent of it to waft through the café and the queue at the cake counter instantly grows longer.

INGREDIENTS

225g margarine
340g soft brown sugar
285g golden syrup
680g plain flour

4 tsp ground ginger
2 tsp bicarbonate of soda
2 eggs

● Put the margarine, sugar and golden syrup into a saucepan and gently heat. Once everything has melted together, add the flour, ginger and bicarbonate of soda.
● Whisk the eggs together in a bowl then stir them into the mixture to form a dough. Wrap this dough in clingfilm and set it aside in the fridge for 1 hour.
● Preheat your oven to 160°C/320°F.
● Once the dough has cooled, roll it out onto a cold surface sprinkled with flour to prevent it from sticking, then cut out your gingerbread man shapes with a cutter.
● Place the gingerbread men onto a baking tray lined with greaseproof paper. Make sure you space them out as they will spread a little during cooking. Bake in the oven for 15 minutes or so.

DORSET APPLE CAKE

SERVES 4

There is no definitive recipe for Dorset apple cake. It's one of those dishes that provokes fierce arguments between villages throughout the county, as everyone seems to believe their way is the only way. The constant in all, of course, is wonderful local apples, baked with butter and sugar to produce a deliciously sticky cake that goes perfectly with Dorset clotted cream. Cut yours into generous slices before serving and make a big pot of tea to sit alongside it on the table.

INGREDIENTS

285g softened butter, plus extra for greasing
6 Bramley apples, peeled, cored and chopped into 1cm pieces
1 lemon, juiced
340g caster sugar, plus extra for sprinkling

2 tsp cinnamon
4 large eggs
450g self-raising flour
Milk
2 tbsp Demerara sugar

● Preheat your oven to 180°C/350°F.

● Take a deep, 30cm cake tin and grease the inside with butter. Line with greaseproof paper and set aside.

● Place the apple pieces in a bowl and toss with the lemon juice. Set aside.

● Cream the butter, caster sugar and cinnamon together in a bowl with an electric whisk until pale and fluffy. Beat in the eggs, one at a time, and whisk in a little of the flour after each egg to keep the mixture smooth. Pour in a little milk to thin it if the consistency becomes too thick.

● Drain the apple pieces and stir them into the mixture.

● Spoon the mixture into the prepared cake tin, gently level the top and sprinkle with the Demerara sugar.

● Bake the cake in the oven for 1 hour or until it has risen and browned on the top (if the cake is getting too brown, you can cover it with a sheet of greaseproof paper after 45 minutes or so). The cake is cooked when you insert a skewer into the centre and it comes out clean.

● Leave the cake to cool in the tin for 10 minutes, then remove and place on a serving plate. Sprinkle generously with caster sugar.

GOOSEBERRY CHEESECAKE

SERVES 8–10

Looking for an unusual take on a classic pud that everyone will love? Our no-bake gooseberry cheesecake is a tangy-sweet, light, summery dessert that will keep in the fridge for up to three days. Get the children to help you make the base – they'll love crushing the biscuits and mixing in the butter. The gooseberries take the edge off the richness of the cheesecake; in our eyes, it's a perfect combination.

INGREDIENTS

400g fresh gooseberries
900g caster sugar
250g ginger biscuits, crushed
115g melted butter

400ml double cream
250g cream cheese
340g condensed milk
4 lemons, juiced

● Put the gooseberries and the sugar into a large saucepan and bring it up to the boil. Let it boil for a few minutes before turning down the heat and letting the mixture simmer for 5 minutes or so, until it takes on a syrupy consistency. Set aside to cool.

● Combine the ginger biscuits with the melted butter in a bowl and mix. Transfer to a cake tin with a removable bottom and press firmly down to create the cheesecake base. Level and set aside.

● Whisk the double cream and cream cheese together until it has the consistency of custard. Add the condensed milk and whisk again before pouring in the lemon juice and whisking for a few seconds more until all the ingredients have combined.

● Spoon this mixture onto the cheesecake base and level. Set aside in the fridge for at least 2 hours to chill and set. When you're ready to serve, remove the cheesecake from the cake tin and spoon over the gooseberry syrup.

MINCEMEAT

MAKES SEVERAL SERVINGS

It just wouldn't be Christmas without mincemeat. How would we at The Hive and The Watch House make our mince pies or Christmas puddings? Much better than the oversweet, supermarket-bought stuff, our mincemeat is of the kind we've been eating in Dorset for hundreds of years – this combination of currants, suet, brandy and spices is, of course, one of the last remnants of medieval cuisine still eaten today – and we're very proud of it. Make up a big batch in time for the festive season and use in puddings or to quickly produce trays of warm pies for those unexpected guests. It will keep in the fridge for up to six months.

INGREDIENTS

250g raisins
375g currants
100ml brandy
1 lemon, juiced and zested
300g shredded suet

250g dark brown sugar
85g chopped mixed peel
½ small nutmeg, grated
1 large Bramley apple, peeled and grated

● Make sure you have plenty of sterilised jars to hand (at The Hive we use kiln jars). The easiest way to get your jars ready is to run them through a dishwasher on the hottest setting.
● Soak the raisins and currants in the brandy and the juice of ½ lemon for at least 1 hour until they are plump and swollen. Drain off the liquid and set aside.
● Combine the raisins and currants with the lemon zest, suet, sugar, mixed peel, nutrmeg and apple (in that order). Mix well. Pour in the retained brandy and stir.
● Spoon the mincemeat into jars and press it down to get rid of any air. Cover and set aside for at least a fortnight before using.

BAKEWELL TART

SERVES 4

The Bakewell tart – a derivation of the original Bakewell pudding – is the result of a happy culinary accident. In the 18th century, a cook at one of the inns in the eponymous Peak District town misheard some recipe instructions and created this delicious combination of almonds and strawberry jam. Her mistake was the world's gain and, even down here on the south coast, there are few rivals to its status as the perfect companion to a cup of tea. These tarts have been selling like – well – hot cakes since we started making them at The Hive Beach Bakery in West Bay.

INGREDIENTS

280g plain flour
500g self-raising flour
225g butter, softened
30g icing sugar
Raspberry jam

450g margarine
450g caster sugar
4 eggs
225g ground almonds
2 tsp almond essence

● First make the pastry. Sift the plain flour and 225g self-raising flour into your bowl, add the butter and rub it in with your fingertips until you have fine breadcrumbs. Stir in the icing sugar and add 2–3 tbsp water to bind the pastry together. Knead the dough lightly on a floured surface, then wrap it in clingfilm and set aside in the fridge for at least 30 minutes.
● Preheat your oven to 180°C/350°F. Roll out the pastry on a floured surface and fill your pastry cases or tart tins. Whether you make several individual tarts or two large ones is totally up to you.
● Blind-bake the tart bases in the oven for 10–15 minutes.
● Spread a layer of raspberry jam onto the base of each tart and set aside.
● Whisk together the margarine, sugar, eggs, ground almonds and the remaining self-raising flour until creamy. Then stir in the almond essence.
● Top up each tart with the almond paste and bake in the oven for 30–40 minutes until the topping turns a golden-brown colour and sets.

MAISY'S CHOCOLATE BOMB

SERVES 4

Maisy, aged 11, is the youngest daughter of Steve Attrill – owner of The Hive and The Watch House – and she's spent her entire life around the cafés. It's no surprise, then, that she should show an interest in cooking and a penchant for creating recipes of her own. And this, her chocolate bomb, is a favourite of the family. Your kids will love it, too, especially if you let them help with the preparation and – afterwards – give them spoons to scrape what's left of the melted chocolate out of the bowl.

INGREDIENTS

165g unsalted butter, plus extra
for greasing
Cocoa powder
165g dark chocolate (70% cocoa solids),
broken into small pieces

3 eggs
3 egg yolks
85g caster sugar
2 tbsp plain flour

● Preheat your oven to 200°C/400°F.
● Take 4 ramekins or pudding moulds, and grease the insides with butter. Sprinkle in a dusting of cocoa powder.
● Bring a saucepan of water up to a gentle simmer. Place the butter and chocolate into a heatproof bowl, and put this on top of the saucepan to create a bain marie. Melt the chocolate and butter, stirring occasionally. Remove from the heat and set aside.
● With an electric whisk, whisk together the eggs, the egg yolks and the sugar until the mixture thickens and takes on a pale colour.
● Carefully fold in the melted chocolate then sift in the flour and gently fold it into the mixture.
● Divide the mixture between the ramekins or pudding moulds and bake in the oven for 10–12 minutes.
● When slightly cooled, turn out the puddings onto plates and serve immediately with a big spoonful of Dorset clotted cream.

PEANUT BRITTLE

SERVES 8–10

A gloriously old-fashioned treat, peanut brittle has been eaten by British children for many a generation and it shows no sign of losing its popularity. Sticky and crunchy at the same time, it is utterly moreish. Make sure you use unsalted nuts in this recipe, though; the last thing you want is an over-the-top combination of sweet and savoury. Children will love stirring the nuts in, and breaking the brittle into little pieces at the end. But it's definitely an adult's job to bring the sugar up past boiling point. You don't have to eat all the brittle straightaway. When put into small bags or boxes, it makes an excellent gift.

INGREDIENTS

2 cups white sugar
200g unsalted peanuts, shelled

200g unsalted mixed nuts (Brazils, almonds, cashews and macadamia)

● Combine the sugar and half a cup of cold water and bring to the boil. Using a sugar thermometer, let the temperature rise to 104°C.
● Mix in the peanuts and any other nuts you choose. Stir well until all have been coated in the sugar mixture.
● Tip the peanut brittle mixture out onto a baking tray lined with greaseproof paper and level with a palette knife. Allow to cool and harden.
● Once the peanut brittle has set, break it into smaller pieces.

LEMON & LIME GINGER LOVELY

SERVES 8–10

This is an impressive, refreshing dessert that is super-quick to make. The sharpness of the citrus fruit perfectly offsets the rich combination of double cream and condensed milk. Crushed ginger biscuits make a delicious spicy-sweet base. Don't forget to get the kids involved in crushing them. Wrap them in a tea towel and bash them with a rolling pin. They'll have never had so much fun in the kitchen.

INGREDIENTS

250g ginger biscuits, crushed
115g melted butter
300ml double cream

170g condensed milk
3 lemons, juiced
2 limes, juiced

● Combine the ginger biscuits with the melted butter in a bowl and mix. Spoon half of the biscuit mixture into serving glasses and set aside.
● Whisk the double cream until it has the consistency of custard. Pour in the condensed milk and whisk again, slowly adding the lemon and lime juice until the mixture is thick and creamy.
● Spoon the mixture into the serving glasses and scatter the remaining ginger biscuits over the top. Chill in the fridge for an hour or so until you are ready to serve.

SCONES

SERVES 8–10

There's nothing that can't be made better by a warm scone and a hot cup of tea. Spread them with butter, or with jam and clotted cream, and the sense of pleasure soars. At The Hive and the Watch House, we sell scones as quickly as our micro-bakery in West Bay can make them. For some people it's a reward at the end of a long beach walk; for others it's the treat around which their afternoon revolves. And for The Hive chefs, it's the thing that makes that post-lunch tea break absolutely perfect.

INGREDIENTS

680g self-raising flour
1 tsp baking powder
225g butter

225g caster sugar
5 eggs
150ml milk

● Preheat your oven to 180°C/350°F.
● Combine the flour, baking powder and butter in a large mixing bowl. Rub the butter in with your fingertips until the mixture resembles fine breadcrumbs.
● Add the sugar and 4 eggs, and mix into the flour mixture with your hands.
● Pour the milk in slowly while continuing to mix. Be careful not to let the mixture get too sticky. You need to achieve a pastry-like texture.
● Tip the dough out onto a cold surface sprinkled with flour to prevent it from sticking. Gently roll it – applying only the minimum of pressure to the rolling pin.
● Use a cutter to cut out the scones. Each should be at least 3cm high.
● Place the scones onto a baking tray lined with greaseproof paper and brush each with a little milk and beaten egg. Bake in the oven for 20–25 minutes.

COCONUT & CHERRY FLAPJACKS

SERVES 8–10

For every family that comes into The Hive or The Watch House for a big meal, there's a dog-walker or beach-stroller that pops in for a quick cup of tea and a cake before continuing their journey. We sell a wide range of sweet treats for this clientele, and our coconut and cherry flapjacks are among the most popular – especially when they're brought direct from the kitchen, still warm and smelling lovely. Children will adore this recipe – and not just the eating part that comes at the end.

INGREDIENTS

225g butter, plus extra for greasing
225g brown sugar
100g golden syrup

255g porridge oats
100g desiccated coconut
100g glacé cherries, chopped

- Preheat your oven to 180°C/350°F.
- Take a deep baking tin and grease the inside with butter. Line with a strip of greaseproof paper and set aside.
- Put the butter, brown sugar and golden syrup into a small saucepan and melt slowly, stirring occasionally, until it reaches a runny consistency.
- Combine the porridge oats, dessicated coconut and cherries in a large bowl and make a well in the centre with the back of a wooden spoon.
- Pour the melted butter mixture into the well and mix well so that all the oats are coated. Spread the mixture into the tin and make it level.
- Put the tin in the oven and bake for 20–25 minutes until the flapjack mixture turns a golden colour.
- Remove from the oven and cut the flapjacks into individual slices while still warm. Turn out of the tin to cool.

STICKY TOFFEE PUDDING

SERVES 8–10

Devilishly delicious, this sticky toffee pudding is the perfect end to a Sunday lunch. A classic British pudding, it is unapologetically sweet, stodgy and, yes, sticky; but this recipe has just the right ratio of pudding to gooey sauce. The dates ensure the finished dessert stays on the right side of heavy and the whole family will adore this indulgent treat with its cascade of sauce. Serve while still steaming from the oven with a big scoop of vanilla ice cream.

INGREDIENTS

195g soft butter
295g soft brown sugar
1 tbsp golden syrup
2 tbsp black treacle
2 eggs

2 tsp vanilla essence
200g self-raising flour
200g dates, pitted
1 tsp bicarbonate of soda
220ml double cream

● Preheat your oven to 180°C/350°F. Line a 60cm baking tin with greaseproof paper.
● Cream 75g butter and 175g sugar together in a large mixing bowl then add in the golden syrup, treacle, eggs and vanilla essence, and mix well. Gently fold in the flour.
● Boil 300ml water and add the dates to this. Let them soak for a few minutes, then pour both the water and dates into a food processor and blitz until the mixture has puréed. Add the bicarbonate of soda and mix.
● Pour the date purée into the flour mixture and stir. Transfer the mixture to the baking tin and bake in the oven for 40 minutes, until it feels springy to the touch. It should also feel slightly sticky.
● While the pudding is cooking, make the toffee sauce. Put the rest of the butter and sugar into a bowl and microwave for a couple of minutes until the butter has melted and the sugar has dissolved. Pour in the double cream and stir, then microwave for another few minutes.
● Divide the pudding between 4 bowls and spoon the toffee sauce over the top. Serve while still warm.

SPICY CARROT CAKE WITH ORANGE ZEST FROSTING

SERVES 8–10

Another insanely popular choice from our puddings and cakes selection at The Hive and The Watch House, our version of the traditional carrot cake – complete with delicious cream cheese-and-orange frosting – sells out almost as quickly as we can make it. A favourite of those who drop in to the cafés for a hot drink and something sweet to fuel their seaside walk, it is made by us from the finest-quality carrots and freshly juiced oranges.

INGREDIENTS

340g soft brown sugar
6 eggs
285g carrots, grated
355ml sunflower oil
170g sultanas
2 oranges, zested and juiced

340g self-raising flour
2 tsp cinnamon
1 tsp mixed spice
2 tsp bicarbonate of soda
500g cream cheese
300g icing sugar

● Preheat your oven to 180°C/350°F.
● Beat the brown sugar and eggs together until light and airy. Add the carrot, sunflower oil, sultanas, and the zest and juice of 1 orange. Mix well. Fold in the flour, cinnamon and mixed spice, and, finally, the bicarbonate of soda. Mix until all the ingredients have been well-combined.
● Pour this batter into a 25cm baking tin. Bake in the oven for 45 minutes until the cake has risen and is springy to the touch. Remove and set aside.
● While the cake is cooling, make the frosting. Put the cream cheese and icing sugar into a food processor and blitz. Mix in the juice of 1 orange.
● Once the cake is cool enough, use a palette knife to apply the frosting to the top. Finish with a sprinkling of orange zest.

CHOCOLATE ST EMILION

SERVES 8–10

Dense and rich, Chocolate St Emilion is a classic. boozy French dessert and those with a sweet tooth will adore this recipe. The macaroons are usually soaked in brandy but our lighter recipe uses Amaretto to give the dish a delicious almond flavour. The chocolate you use is crucial – it should be high-quality and consist of at least 70 per cent cocoa solids. Try decorating with chocolate curls (you'll need a vegetable peeler and a room-temperature bar of chocolate) and serve with thick double cream.

INGREDIENTS

150g macaroons
Amaretto
110g butter
250g dark chocolate (70% cocoa solids),
broken into small pieces

200ml milk
110g caster sugar
1 egg yolk

● Soak the macaroons in 2–3 tbsp Amaretto for a few minutes. Don't leave them in for too long or they'll go soggy. Place the Amaretto-soaked macaroons into a serving dish or individual serving glasses.

● Bring a saucepan of water up to a gentle simmer. Place the butter and chocolate into a heatproof bowl, and put this on top of the saucepan to create a bain marie. Melt the chocolate and butter, stirring occasionally. Once melted, add the milk and sugar. Mix well.

● Remove the mixture from the heat and gently whisk in the egg yolk until the chocolate begins to shine.

● Pour the chocolate mixture over the macaroons and set aside in the fridge for 2–3 hours to chill and set. Remove from the fridge 30 minutes before serving.

THE HIVE HOMEMADE DOG BISCUITS

SERVES LOTS OF DOGS

This wouldn't be a proper family cookbook without us including at least one recipe for the canine members of the household. Dogs are some of The Hive's most important customers. And with the beach just yards from our door and the famous southwest coastal path winding right past the café, we get a huge number of them leading their owners through our door. While those humans tuck into everything from slices of cake to enormous seafood platters, there's been nothing for the pets to eat – until now.

INGREDIENTS

355g spelt flour
415g strong brown flour
2 tbsp brown sugar
4 tbsp brown linseeds

3 tbsp powdered milk
3 eggs
240ml vegetable oil

● Preheat your oven to 170°C/325°F.
● Combine the spelt flour and the brown flour in a large bowl. Add the brown sugar, linseeds, powdered milk and a pinch of salt, and mix well.
● Beat the eggs into the mixture, then add the vegetable oil and stir. If the consistency of the mixture is too thick, add a little water to loosen it.
● Roll the mixture out to about 3cm thick onto a cold surface sprinkled with flour to prevent it from sticking, then cut it into dog biscuit shapes.
● Place the dog biscuits onto a baking tray lined with greaseproof paper (you can put them close together as they won't spread during cooking) and bake for 40 minutes or so until firm.

INDEX

A

almonds: sweet & spicy nuts **92**; Bakewell tart **220**; peanut brittle **224**

almond essence: Bakewell tart **220**

Amaretto: chocolate St Emilion **236**

apples: apple & mustard sausage rolls **72**; Ashley Chase cheeseboard with pineapple chutney **86**; Dorset apple cake **214**; mincemeat **218**

asparagus: crab, asparagus & pomegranate salad **50**; pulled pork pizza **160**

aubergines: trio of red mullet, grey mullet & John Dory **144**

avocados: crayfish, prawn & avocado salad sandwich **78**; ham & pineapple pizza with a twist **170**

B

bacon: tall pancake stack with crispy bacon **22**; eggy bread with streaky bacon **28**; messy bacon ciabatta **40**; stargazy pie **154**

basil: Thai king prawn soup **64**; tray-baked salmon with olives & tomatoes **108**; trio of red mullet, grey mullet & John Dory **144**

bay leaves: pea & ham soup with mint creme fraîche **60**; baked gilthead bream with herbs & garlic **112**; fish & saffron stew **118**; pulled pork pizza **160**; smoked haddock & potato pizza **174**

beansprouts: sashimi of beef with teriyaki sauce **80**

beef: sashimi of beef with teriyaki sauce **80**; surf & turf sandwich **96**; surf & turf **150**; chargrilled steak & balsamic red onion pizza **172**; teriyaki beef & lettuce parcels **198**

beetroot: the maverick pizza **176**

black pudding: pan-fried scallops with pancetta & black pudding **36**

blueberries: blueberry pancakes with fresh fruit & vanilla mascarpone **38**

brandy: mincemeat **218**

Brazil nuts: sweet & spicy nuts **92**; peanut brittle **224**

bread: eggy bread with streaky bacon **28**; scrambled rhea's egg served in the shell **30**; messy bacon ciabatta **40**; lobster ciabatta **68**; fish bap with aïoli **74**; crayfish, prawn & avocado salad sandwich **78**; sardine pâté served with Melba toast **82**; Weymouth brown crab sandwich **90**; Dorset Blue Vinney, walnut & wild rocket sandwich **94**; surf & turf sandwich **96**; hot-smoked salmon with dill crème fraîche **98**; shrimp burgers with lemon mayonnaise **186**; crab salsa crostini **200**; fish dogs **202**

breadcrumbs: salmon Scotch eggs **88**; stargazy pie **154**; fish dogs **202**

butter: tall pancake stack with crispy bacon **22**; bubble & squeak **24**; scrambled rhea's egg served in the shell **30**; smoked haddock frittata **34**; blueberry pancakes with fresh fruit & vanilla mascarpone **38**; messy bacon ciabatta **40**; mussel & saffron soup **44**; leek & potato soup with smoked mackerel **48**; pea & ham soup with mint creme fraîche **60**; apple & mustard sausage rolls **72**; crayfish, prawn & avocado salad sandwich **78**; sardine pâté served with Melba toast **82**; Weymouth brown crab sandwich **90**; Dorset Blue Vinney, walnut & wild rocket sandwich **94**; whole Dover sole with lemon butter sauce **106**; grilled fillet of coley with smoked garlic mash **110**; seabass

with sorrel sauce & crispy new potatoes **114**; grilled fillet of cod with spinach & butter sauce **120**; chargrilled lobster with herb butter **128**; pan-fried scallops with truffle mash & crispy pancetta **130**; wild halibut with samphire & lobster butter **134**; hot shellfish in a wood sorrel dressing **138**; large turbot with a light fish sauce **140**; sticky king prawns **142**; turbot steak with pancetta & cava cream sauce **146**; whole roasted halibut with pan-fried scallops **148**; the Pisces pizza **164**; wild mushroom, spinach & soft poached egg pizza **178**; hot & cold seafood platter **182**; chocolate & cherry tiffin **208**; Dorset apple cake **214**; gooseberry cheesecake **216**; Bakewell tart **220**; Maisy's chocolate bomb **222**; lemon & lime ginger lovely **226**; scones **228**; coconut & cherry flapjacks **230**; sticky toffee pudding **232**; chocolate St Emilion **236**
butternut squash: roasted butternut squash, courgette & feta pizza **162**;

C

capers: The Chesil Smokery salmon board **76**; salmon Scotch eggs **88**; whole roasted halibut with pan-fried scallops **148**
carrots: sashimi of beef with teriyaki sauce **80**; fish & saffron stew **118**; spicy carrot cake with orange zest frosting **234**
cashew nuts: sweet & spicy nuts **92**; peanut brittle **224**
cauliflower: cauliflower soup with curried scallops **52**
cava: turbot steak with pancetta & cava cream sauce **146**
cayenne pepper: sardine pâté served with Melba toast **82**
cheddar: bubble & squeak **24**; smoked haddock

frittata **34**; messy bacon ciabatta **40**; Ashley Chase cheeseboard with pineapple chutney **86**; surf & turf **150**; chorizo & roasted red pepper pizza **158**; pulled pork pizza **160**; roasted butternut squash, courgette & feta pizza **162**; the Pisces pizza **164**; ham & pineapple pizza with a twist **170**; chargrilled steak & balsamic red onion pizza **172**; smoked haddock & potato pizza **174**; the maverick pizza **176**; wild mushroom, spinach & soft poached egg pizza **178**; large fish pie **194**
cherries: chocolate & cherry tiffin **208**; coconut & cherry flapjacks **230**
chervil: large turbot with a light fish sauce **140**
chicken: paella **190**
chicken stock: cauliflower soup with curried scallops **52**; haddock & white bean soup **56**; Thai king prawn soup **64**; paella **190**
chillies: Thai king prawn soup **64**; ceviche of bream **70**; sashimi of beef with teriyaki sauce **80**; seabass fillet with mango & chilli salsa **122**; squid with roasted red peppers & olives **126**; roasted seabass with rosemary & confit lemons **132**; seabass en papillote with Thai flavours **152**; chorizo & roasted red pepper pizza **158**; roasted butternut squash, courgette & feta pizza **162**; ham & pineapple pizza with a twist **170**; shrimp burgers with lemon mayonnaise **186**; king prawn & monkfish skewers **188**; teriyaki beef & lettuce parcels **198**; king prawn curry **204**
chives: smoked haddock frittata **34**; leek & potato soup with smoked mackerel **48**; whole Dover sole with lemon butter sauce **106**; grilled fillet of cod with spinach & butter sauce **120**; seabass fillet with mango & chilli salsa **122**; chargrilled lobster with herb butter **128**; wild halibut with samphire & lobster butter **134**; smoked haddock & potato pizza **174**; the maverick pizza **176**; large fish pie **194**
chocolate: chocolate & cherry tiffin **208**; Maisy's

D

M

NOTES

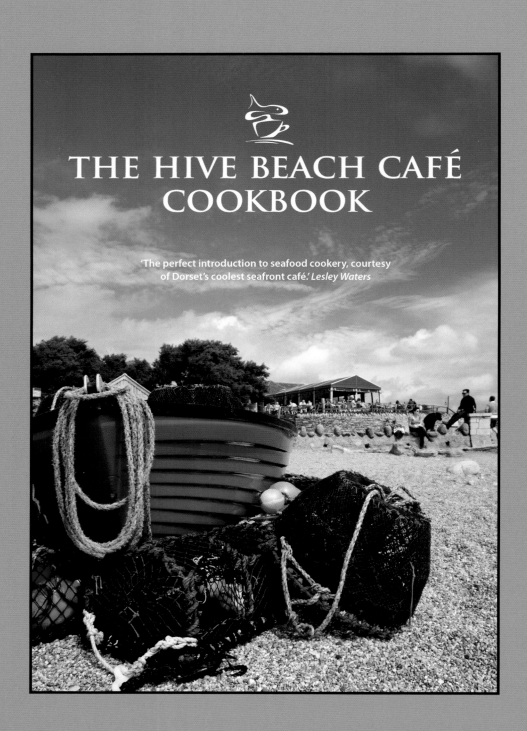

ALSO AVAILABLE

THE HIVE BEACH CAFÉ COOKBOOK

'Simple, unfussy dining from the Dorset hotspot with the fantastic view.' Mark Hix

'What a lovely book, full of clean and simple recipes. You can almost smell the food mingled with a warm sea breeze coming from the pages.' Valentine Warner

'The Hive Beach Café is a proper seafood venue, and I love these simple and beautiful recipes that I could honestly eat time after time.' Mitch Tonks

Loved by the likes of AA Gill, Jasper Conran and Rick Stein – not to mention its loyal, local clientele – The Hive Beach Café in Burton Bradstock, West Dorset, has been at the forefront of Britain's burgeoning beach café scene for several years now. Serving stunning seasonal seafood in a relaxed and informal setting just yards from the sea, it has become one of Dorset's coolest foodie destinations.

The Hive Beach Café Cookbook features more than 100 fish and seafood recipes divided into four seasons. It reflects The Hive's chefs' passion for sustainability and protecting our dwindling fish stocks. You're just as likely to discover recipes for coley, cuttlefish, garfish, gurnard and huss as you are to come across innovative new ways to cook lobster, scallops and squid.

£16.99, BRISTLEBIRD BOOKS
WWW.HIVECOOKBOOK.CO.UK

THE HIVE BEACH CAFÉ

WWW.HIVEBEACHCAFE.CO.UK